Reluctant Revolutionaries
A Century of Head Mistresses 1874-1974

Reluctant Revolutionaries

A Century of Head Mistresses 1874-1974

Written for the Association of Head Mistresses by
NONITA GLENDAY and MARY PRICE

Foreword by the Rt. Hon. Lord Butler of Saffron Walden

Pitman Publishing

First published 1974
Reprinted in paperback 1975

Sir Isaac Pitman and Sons Ltd
Pitman House, Parker Street, Kingsway, London WC2B 5PB
Banda Street, PO Box 46038, Nairobi, Kenya
Pitman Publishing Pty Ltd
Pitman House, 158 Bouverie Street, Carlton, Victoria 3053, Australia
Pitman Publishing Corporation
6 East 43rd Street, New York, NY 10017, USA
Sir Isaac Pitman (Canada) Ltd
495 Wellington Street West, Toronto 135, Canada
The Copp Clark Publishing Company
517 Wellington Street West, Toronto 135, Canada

ISBN: 0 273 00117 5

Reproduced and printed by photolithography and bound in
Great Britain at The Pitman Press, Bath
G4619: 11

Foreword

It seems quite strange today to think of Head Mistresses as revolutionaries, or, as Lucy Savill of Lincoln High School wrote, "by no means tame or tameable." She is right to say that the first Heads were mostly people of strong spiritual conviction impelling them to serve their generation. She is right to go on to say that the first schools were as different as flowers are in a garden through the expression of the personality of their first Heads, women of culture and intellectual power. The names of Frances Mary Buss, Dorothea Beale and Mary Eliza Porter come to mind as being the protagonists of the struggle to create girls' education as we know it today after a hundred years. Now women are pressing to take their places in men's colleges, the wheel has turned full circle and it is now socially progressive to have girls in the senior forms of Public Schools, originally created for boys. It is fascinating to me whose great uncle, when Master of Harrow, attended one of the first boys' Head Masters' affairs at Uppingham in 1864, to see that the Head Mistresses also held an early meeting in Uppingham. There is no wonder that the name Thring is so celebrated in the history of adolescent education.

This history of one hundred years traces girls' education through the two world wars and I am quoted as remarking that educational progress has by an extraordinary coincidence coincided with periods of war: 1870, 1902 (end of the Boer war), 1918, 1941-44—all these periods are referred to.

The book makes clear that women co-operated with the Fleming Committee set up to examine the future of Public Schools; alas the results were not important. The book refers to girls' participation in the move forward of secondary education for all and remarks that at the time of the passing of the Act of 1944 the Head Mistresses favoured the raising of the school-leaving age to sixteen. It seems strange that at the date I write we have not yet reached that goal. However idiosyncratic Winston Churchill's views might have been about education, he was in favour of raising the school-leaving age to sixteen, on the advice of his then young daughter Mary, who was serving in the forces.

There is an interesting chapter about the movement towards compulsory comprehensive education and references to the Act of 1944 having started off on a tripartite basis. I foresaw in the White Paper in 1943 that all aspects of secondary education could be under one roof but this book is right in stating that it was the Norwood Report which started things off. Now at any rate the comprehensive idea has taken hold, and has fallen within the framework of the Act itself. E. Halévy, of immortal memory, described the first girls' education as "a social revolution of the first magnitude." Certainly this excellent volume, with its devoted tributes to the founders, makes this revolution seem worth while and the amazing list of members at the Uppingham Conference of 1887 may feel that their leadership has not been in vain.

I personally hold that girls' secondary education will be justified on its own and not necessarily by co-educational experiment. I think much of the fight of the founders was originally designed to be directed to this end but this is a matter of opinion.

I cannot, in conclusion, too strongly recommend the initiative and energy with which this book has been prepared.

Trinity College,
Cambridge.

Preface

This is not an official history of the Association of Head Mistresses nor is it a policy statement. In 1970 the President, Beryl Williams, suggested that something should be written to commemorate the centenary in 1974. The Executive Committee then commissioned a team of Life Members—Nonita Glenday, Eileen Harold, Hannah Lister and Mary Price—to go through the Association's archives, and from them and other sources to write as they wished. A great deal of research had been done by the team when Eileen Harold had to give up because of illness, and Beryl Williams replaced her.

It is never easy to write as a team, and problems of distance and the personal and professional commitments of busy women had to be overcome before Nonita Glenday and Mary Price could get down to the bulk of the writing. They are greatly indebted to those responsible for the Association's archives and the archives of many girls' schools; the Bodleian; the libraries of the Department of Education and Science and the Department of Health and Social Security; the British Museum; *Punch*; members of Her Majesty's Inspectorate; the staffs of local education authorities; and members of other associations of teachers as well as of their own. All these were invaluable sources of information. The team could not have worked effectively without the generous hospitality of head mistresses, particularly at St Mary's Convent, Ascot, and of University College Hospital Medical School.

Christopher Price has written of schools: "Not that much radical change takes place. Most heads like things as they are." *Reluctant Revolutionaries* suggests that, whatever head mistresses may like, revolutionaries many have been. In one hundred years their schools have developed from secondary schools for a very few middle-class girls, through schools for all the academically able, towards the goal of real opportunity for full secondary education for all. We are indeed grateful to the authors of this book who show that before each step forward there have been head mistresses confidently pointing the way for the more apprehensive to follow. We know that traditions if they are to flourish must, like all living organisms, be adaptable to change. Such knowledge augurs well for the next hundred years.

Jean Wilks
President of the Association of Head Mistresses

Acknowledgements

In her preface the President has indicated the range of sources from which we were able to draw material for this book. We should like particularly to emphasize our indebtedness to our colleagues in the Association, many of whom allowed us to use records and publications which were invaluable, and who were always ready to listen, discuss and encourage. Dr Jan Milburn's thesis, "The Secondary Schoolmistress, 1895-1914," also provided us with much useful information.

We are specially grateful to Miss D.M. Jepson, Chief Librarian to the Department of Education and Science, who welcomed us to the library when she herself was engaged in organizing the monumental task of moving it to Queen Elizabeth House; to Miss Spalding and Miss West who responded with inexhaustible patience to repeated—and often inconvenient—requests for documents, minute books, and other massive tomes from the office; to Mrs Boyce who typed and retyped the manuscript, apparently undismayed by eccentricities of handwriting and intricate revisions; to Mr Malcolm Pendrill who gave such great care to photographing documents and other illustrative material; and to Mr David Lamb for his original and apposite drawings.

Contents

Illustrations

Chapter 1

Nine worthies

It is the year 1874 and the scene is Myra Lodge, a Victorian house in Primrose Hill, Camden, which is occupied by the boarders of the North London Collegiate School and is also the residence of the head mistress. A four-wheeler draws up at the entrance, and from it steps a young woman, slight and attractive in appearance, dressed discreetly but fashionably, and carrying a reticule which holds not only her purse but also a notebook and pencil. She looks about her with an air of alert observation, pays the cabman, pulls the door-bell, and the door is opened by a trim parlour-maid who shows her into a pleasant, sunny drawing-room where eight other ladies are already assembled.

This is the first meeting of the Association of Head Mistresses, and these are the pioneers. Who are they? The latest comer is Elizabeth Day of Manchester High School; the hostess and convener is Frances Mary Buss of the North London Collegiate School; Dorothea Beale of Cheltenham Ladies' College takes the chair and the other six are:

Selina Hadland, Milton Mount College, Gravesend;
Elsie Day, Grey Coat Hospital, Westminster;
Harriet Morant Jones, Notting Hill High School;
Marion Elford, The Camden School;
C.C. Derrick, St Martin's Middle Class School, London;
Mary Eliza Porter, Chelsea High School.

By 1874 the movement for girls' education was gathering

momentum, and this little group of women, quiet and unassuming as one might at first sight suppose them to be, were really nothing of the kind. They were dauntless, indefatigable and compounded of fibre as tough as that of any heroine who made her name by scaling the Alps or exploring the desert. A number of schools for girls had come into existence since the 1860s, and situations were beginning to arise which had no precedent but needed to be wisely handled. Head mistresses sometimes "lived and worked in strange conditions of isolation" and it was important for them to meet each other, exchange views and compare their ideas. They had to arrive at a common policy on such matters of principle as the right of the head mistress to appoint and dismiss staff, her control over the choice of books and determination of methods, and other nice points of adjustment concerning the powers of the head mistress and those of the governing body. There was also the question of how to find and train even the minimum number of teachers; and there were many other knotty problems. In September 1874 Frances Mary Buss wrote to a friend saying that the time had come "to form an Association of Head Mistresses, and hold occasional conferences, in order to know what we ought to assert and what surrender"—a most revealing phrase. So, on 22 December 1874, this little group of nine women met, and the Association of Head Mistresses came into existence.

Before this a series of significant events had taken place, gradually opening up the way. In 1848 Queen's College, Harley Street, was founded and "planned to provide advanced education for women and training for teachers and governesses, both in day and evening classes." In 1854, when the age of admission was fixed at fourteen, a school was attached, with women teachers for younger girls. In 1849 Bedford College was founded to "provide for young ladies at a moderate expense a curriculum of general education on the same plan as the public Universities"—in fact, a college for higher education, not a school. It was at one or other of these establishments that many of the pioneers had received their education or been on the staff. A small incident connected with Bedford College deserves notice. In 1851 a scholarship fund was instituted and the sum of twenty pounds was received from the Reverend Edwin Chapman of Ashley Hill, Bristol: the Principal, Mrs Reid, noted,

"Insignificant as this is, it deserves commemoration as being the only instance, as far as I can learn, of a gentleman giving more than ten pounds to promote the higher education of women."

In 1863 Cambridge allowed girls to attempt the Cambridge Local Examination as an unofficial experiment, this being largely due to the efforts of Emily Davies, the founder of Girton; and in 1865 "a bold step was taken" when girls as well as boys were formally admitted to the Local Examination, on condition that their results should not be published. *The Saturday Review* commented, "The most curious development . . . is a proposal . . . for submitting young ladies to Local University examinations. The idea almost takes one's breath away." Fortunately some people had enough breath left to confirm the admission of girls as a permanent arrangement in 1867.

The year 1864 saw the appointment of the Schools Inquiry Commission under the chairmanship of Lord Taunton to survey the field of secondary education for girls, as well as boys, before which Frances Mary Buss, Dorothea Beale and the indefatigable Mary Eliza Porter gave evidence. Mary Eliza Porter had a really astonishing career, and seems to have specialized in the opening and organization of girls' schools. Between the years 1871 and 1880 she was principal of a Training College in Tiverton, the first head mistress of Drake and Tonson's School, Keighley, (later Keighley Girls' Grammar School), Chelsea High School, Bradford Girls' School and Bedford Modern School. She was a leading figure at a conference on teacher training held at the College of Preceptors in 1872. A former pupil of Bradford wrote in their Jubilee Record, "We thought a great deal of our practical, able head mistress, Miss Porter. She gave Scripture lessons in Class I and frequently read us with great expression extracts from the poets. On Friday mornings she gave addresses to the whole school. We also had Swedish drill under her in the gymnasium."

The year 1864 was important in the North of England, for in that year, spurred on by the zeal of Anne Jemima Clough and Josephine Butler, the North of England Council for Promoting the Higher Education of Women was established, with far-reaching results. It was formed to counteract "the unwise and painful disproportion between the supply of schools for girls and the supply for boys." In Elizabeth Day's words, "There were many schools for girls and there were good schools, but the many were not good and the good were not many."

The whole movement for girls' education must be seen not as an isolated event but as one manifestation of rebellion amongst women of character and intelligence who could no longer tolerate the vapid, frivolous life in which so many of them were expected to find satisfaction. Individuals had already broken through in various fields and by the 1850s a small number of these had achieved recognition of their work. There were Caroline Sheridan, who fought for the rights of married women, Mary Somerville, a leading writer on scientific subjects, two philanthropists—Mary Carpenter, who founded Kingswood as a Boys' Reformatory in Bristol, and Louisa Twining, the workhouse reformer, and, at the peak, Elizabeth Garrett Anderson, the first woman to qualify as a doctor in England. An early champion of girls' education was Barbara Leigh Smith, one of the first students at Bedford College; she and her husband, Dr Bodichon, were later to have a great influence on the development of the movement.

It is difficult for us to realize how barren and frustrating a woman's life could be in the prosperous nineteenth century, and how limited her horizon. Frances Power Cobbe, the philanthropist and social worker, said of her school, "That a pupil in that school should become an artist or authoress would have been regarded as a deplorable dereliction. Not that which was good or useful to the community, or even that which could be delightful to ourselves [was encouraged] but only that which would make us admired in society...." The evidence given by Emily Davies before the Taunton Commission contained the words, "The ideal presented to a young girl is to be amiable, unoffensive, always ready to give pleasure, and to be pleased," and another piece of evidence ran, "There is a long-established and inveterate prejudice, though it may not often be distinctly expressed, that girls are less capable of mental cultivation, and less in need of it, than boys: that accomplishments and what is showy and superficially attractive are what is really essential." James Bryce, then one of the assistant commissioners, summed it up when he wrote in his section of the Report, "Although the world has now existed for several thousand years the notion

Pioneers
(From The Ladies, October 1872)

that women have minds as cultivable and worth cultivating as men's minds is still regarded by the ordinary British parent as an offensive, not to say a revolutionary, paradox."

The women's magazines of the period give a very fair idea of the interests generally accepted as suitable for a woman of the middle classes. In addition to serial fiction and articles on home management they reveal a quite extraordinary preoccupation with dress, advice being given on suitable outfits for Morning Toilet, Visiting Costume, Walking Costume, Indoor Costume, Dinner or Reception Toilet, Travelling Dress and Costumes for the Country; also for bonnets and hats of every description, and for every age from babyhood to the elderly lady. One of the most popular journals was *The Ladies*, containing as regular features a section headed "Twitterings" and another "Marriages in High Life"; any mention of serious subjects was obviously taboo. Gradually, however, a different note creeps in, showing the new influences at work, and education for women and girls actually becomes news. On 26 April 1872 there is the report of a lecture given by Sophia Jex-Blake on the Medical Education of Women. In June appears a dissertation on the Education of Girls, and mention of the National Union for improving the education of women. This is followed by a notice of the Cambridge Examination for Women, giving the address of the local secretary in Rugby, and a record of the numbers of successful candidates for four consecutive years: "1869: 36, 1870: 84, 1871: 126, 1872: 154." On 28 September there is a "Ladies New Book List," mentioning two books on Geometry and Algebra, and such items soon became more frequent.

A new conception of girls' education was becoming accepted as a fundamental need of society. Probably the movement gained impetus from the dawning realization in the country as a whole of the total lack of education of many of its citizens. There were in existence the famous public schools, almost entirely boarding, for sons of the well-to-do, and a variety of private schools for boys or girls, some better than others, but of which the one attended by Frances Power Cobbe is a typical example. For the children of the masses there were only the denominational schools until the great Education Act of 1870 began the task of "filling the gaps" by enabling local authorities to set up School Boards to provide schools from rate aid, but it

Pupils
(From The Ladies, December 1872)

was unthinkable for a girl from a middle-class home to attend one of these and she was in fact in a worse plight than her poorer sister.

It is interesting to look into the early years and education of the founders of the Association of Head Mistresses and see how they succeeded in realizing their ambitions. First, of course, there is the founder, Frances Mary Buss. She was born in 1827 into a professional family, the eldest of ten children and the only girl. Her father, Robert William Buss, was an artist and etcher of recognized talent. Her mother, Frances Buss, in spite of the cares of her family, went to classes at the Home and Colonial Institute and in 1845 opened a small private school, known as the Pestalozzian School, in Clarence Road, Kentish Town. Frances Mary went as a pupil to Mrs Wyard's private school in Hampstead Road, and stayed on as a teacher. She says of herself, "After I reached my fourteenth birthday I began to teach. I was in sole charge for a week at a time when I was sixteen, and never since have I spent my days out of a school-room." In 1845 she joined her mother in the Clarence Road venture and held morning classes for young ladies on the same premises. The prospectus stated, "The course of Education will combine the usual accomplishments with the essential points of a liberal education." She added to her own education by attending evening classes at Queen's College, where she gained certificates in French, German and Geography. In 1849 the dual school moved to Holmes Terrace, and in 1850 the North London Collegiate School was opened in the family house in Camden Street.

Teaching must have been in the blood, and it is clear that much of her education came from her father and mother, and the background of an intellectual and cultural family life. Indeed the North London Collegiate School began as a family venture; Frances Mary was the head mistress, Mrs Buss took the younger pupils and Mr Buss taught Science, Elocution and Drawing. A brother, Alfred, took classes in Arithmetic and Latin, and even young Septimus helped.

Frances Mary Buss was a great personality, possessing the qualities of a true pioneer and originator. She created a school which, in her own lifetime, was to become a model for girls' education, studied and visited by educators who came not only to see the school but to consult the head mistress and benefit from her guidance and advice. Her success owed much to her singleness of purpose and to her capacity for assimilating new ideas. "Somebody must begin things," she said. Sophie Bryant speaks of her active brain and "extraordinary energy of will. She was careful and deliberate in forming ideas, but an idea in her mind began to realize itself in action as soon as it was formed. Never in haste to decide, always swift, and still more sure, to act." Many who knew her have mentioned her generosity of mind and action, the absence of personal ambition, and the delight she took in the pleasures and distinctions of others. Her influence was felt throughout the educational world where she played a leading part, showing the same enterprise and astonishing industry as in her school.

Dorothea Beale, the other moving spirit in the founding of the Association, had a different upbringing. Her father was a London surgeon, and she had a prosperous family background. She was educated first by governesses, afterwards at a boarding school, and then spent some years at home "helping her schoolboy brothers, taking up—with the help of visiting teachers—various subjects in succession," attending lectures and studying music. She said that "the only really inspiring teaching" she had in her girlhood was the informal sort obtained from the reading and conversation of family life. At the age of sixteen she spent a year at a school in Paris, and on her return "threw herself with joy into the Queen's College lectures and examinations." She studied mathematics and classics, and was appointed to the staff, "first as mathematical and afterwards also as classical tutor." From there she went to be head of Casterton School, Carnforth, leaving in 1858 when she was appointed head mistress of Cheltenham Ladies' College, a day school with three boarding houses. It had been in existence for four years, but after a successful start the numbers had dropped and the principal had resigned. The re-creation of Cheltenham was to be Dorothea Beale's life-work. The first two years were a struggle against prejudice and ignorance, plagued by anxiety over numbers and unsound finances, but gradually she established confidence and brought about a change. At the end of five years a transformation had taken place, and the school was to become one of the most famous of girls' boarding schools, known all over the world.

Dorothea Beale was an intellectual, and deeply religious. As a girl she was sensitive and serious-minded and is said "never to have learnt to play." Her life was strictly disciplined, and, although she developed powers as a practical woman of affairs, she remained at heart an idealist. She was educating girls of the upper middle class, and often said to them "that a life not lived in some sense as a working life was a neglect to pay the rent we owe for our existence." Lilian Faithfull, her successor, wrote that "there was nothing accidental about her work. It was marked by independence, conviction, principle, and the mind of the great dictator was everywhere perceptible."

Much has been written elsewhere about these two pioneers of girls' education, remarkable characters both. There are others, less well-known, whose lives are worth recounting, showing as they do that only women of exceptional intelligence and determination could surmount the obstacles in their way and stay the course. A good example is Elizabeth Day of Manchester. She was born in 1844, at 10 Upper Thames Street in the City of London. Her father was a managing clerk to a Government coal contractor, and they lived in a delightful old house on the river, up and down which the coal was carried. With the coming of railways this traffic ceased and the family moved to the West End, a change which they considered a great deprivation. From the age of ten to fourteen years, Elizabeth went to a little day-school in South Molton Street, and then spent a short time at a "very peculiar Boarding School" in Rugby. Her mother and five aunts had all been private governesses, but undeterred by that she said that she could not "remember a time when she did not look forward to a life as a teacher." At the age of fourteen she taught in a Sunday School class, and she had in all seven years' experience as a private governess, covering ten different families. At the same time she was having lessons in Italian, Latin, Drawing and German, and reading many standard English books with her mother. She always maintained that she learnt far more from her parents than from any of her school-teachers.

At the age of seventeen she went to Queen's College, for German only, and five years later became a pupil-teacher there.

"Thus," she says, "began a new life for me." The lecturers and the library proved a turning point in her career. She had saved enough from her work as governess to cover her expenses at the College, but from 1867 to 1873 she had to return to private teaching, though she still attended some classes and was appointed tutor in Greek. These years must have been very arduous, for in her account of them she says, "Three days a week I was out, either learning or teaching, from 8 a.m. to 7 p.m. Two days from 8.0 to 6.0 and on Saturdays I came home about 3.0." In 1871 she entered for the Cambridge Women's Examinations, by then firmly established, her fees being paid by a friend. For some time she lived with friends in Rugby and joined classes arranged for young women, staffed by masters from Rugby School. On her results in the Cambridge Examination she was offered a scholarship to Merton Hall, Cambridge (later Newnham College), but could not afford to take it up. Instead, she followed correspondence classes for the language and moral sciences group, and won a prize of thirty pounds to be spent on books, and a gratuity of five pounds.

In 1873 she was in Rugby, taking the Cambridge Examination, when Mrs Kitchener, the local secretary, told her of a girls' school to be opened in Manchester and asked her to apply for the post of head mistress. Twice she said "No, thank you," politely but quite firmly, but eventually she relented and went to Manchester to meet the Provisional Committee, who appointed her as the first head mistress of Manchester High School. She is said to have been "quick-witted and nimble-minded, with unlimited power and love for continuous, rapid work."

It was to make life more tolerable for girls such as these, and to give them the opportunities for which they longed, that the girls' schools of the 1860s and 1870s were created, and through all the uncertainties and misrepresentations of these and the ensuing years the pioneers preserved a steady sense of purpose and never lost sight of the main issues. It is a mistake to think that their primary objective was to imitate or vie with men; some of them felt that it was essential to insist that girls should be allowed to take the same examinations as boys, and be assessed on exactly the same standards, because it was the only way to prove their case, namely that the mental capacity of girls was not inferior to that of boys; but even amongst themselves there were different shades of opinion on this, and from the first they stressed the desirability of womanliness and recognized that the curriculum for boys and girls need not be identical. People sometimes comment on the fact that Saturday morning school was for many years the accepted practice in boys' day-schools, but very seldom in girls', not realizing that this was the result of considered deliberation, for in 1878 the Association discussed the matter at a Conference and stated that "the idea of Saturday morning school for day pupils must be rejected, because there must be no suggestion that the girls were being prevented from helping their mothers in week-end shopping and other domestic tasks."

The pioneers themselves certainly retained their womanly qualities. They were often anxious, perturbed and strained by the efforts they had to make, the breaking of new ground, and the publicity they could not avoid, but their courage never failed. There is an account of one occasion when Emily Davies and Frances Mary Buss had been invited to give oral evidence to the Taunton Commission in November 1865. Emily Davies went in first and "throughout the ordeal showed no signs of strain, although later she confessed to nervousness. Frances Mary Buss followed, and Emily Davies was comfortably relaxing with claret and biscuits in the secretary's room when Dyke Acland, one of the commissioners, came hurrying in saying, 'This witness is not so self-possessed as the other,' and asked her to go back to support Frances Mary Buss. Frances Mary was almost speechless with nervousness, but she managed to give good answers to questions." Her display of anxiety was more of a help than a hindrance, for the commissioners warmed to this expression of female frailty.

The Association was formed for mutual support and guidance, and these it has offered to its members ever since its foundation. Indeed, the future pattern of girls' secondary school education was to depend to a remarkable extent on the decisions made by this little group and their adherents. The phrase "what to assert and what to surrender" recognizes that, from the first, new ideas had to be formulated and prejudices overcome, and the same necessity has occurred again and again in the history of the Association. Revolution was at times the only course, and the natural reluctance felt by individuals in carrying it out was often only overcome by the reassurance given from the Association as a whole.

One revolutionary concept asserted from the beginning was that the head mistresses of all types of public secondary schools for girls should belong to the same association. Its original title was The Association of Head Mistresses of Endowed and Proprietary Schools, and membership was to be open to head mistresses "not only of First Grade Schools, but of Schools of Second and even Third Grade." (These were the categories into which the Taunton Commission had divided the schools which provided education for children of "the middle and higher classes.") As different types of schools developed, so the membership became increasingly varied, but there has never been a division corresponding to that between the Head Masters' Conference and the Incorporated Association of Head Masters. Even among the nine schools represented at Myra Lodge in 1874, there was considerable diversity.

The North London Collegiate School was primarily a day school, conscious of "a call to educate the daughters of the neglected middle classes." It prided itself on producing within the school a classless society with no barrier of religion or rank. An ex-pupil has said "No one asked you who you were or where you came from" and "it was a matter of honour to make your clothes last as long as possible." Cheltenham Ladies' College, on the other hand, was founded for the daughters and young children of noblemen and gentlemen in Cheltenham, and it made a suitable start in Cambridge House, which had been the temporary residence of the Duke of Wellington. It recognized that "a due cultivation of women's minds is not only desirable in itself but the general welfare of society at large depends on it," but it was very select; references were required from parents and no daughters of tradespeople were admitted.

Milton Mount College was opened in 1873 as a boarding school for the daughters of Congregational Ministers; it "incorporated the most up-to-date features with stress on light and air as conducive to work and health." The letter of appointment to Selina Hadland, the first head mistress, stated, "We aim to establish an institution which shall be the opposite of a fashionable boarding school. We wish to give, not a superficial but a solid and thorough, education, to train the pupils to love unselfish work and Christian virtues, to honour labour and to cultivate independence of feeling," and on the opening day the head mistress stated that "no prizes would be given. The luxury of acquiring knowledge is its own reward."

The Grey Coat Hospital is one of the most famous of the old Charity Foundations, established in 1698 by "eight worthy citizens of Westminster" for forty poor children, boys and girls. In 1873 a new scheme was drawn up and a secondary day-school for girls provided in the original buildings. These were almost completely destroyed by the blitz in 1941, but in spite of all the difficulties it has had to face the school still flourishes in Westminster, holding the status of a voluntary aided school.

Chelsea High School was the first and Notting Hill the second of the schools founded by the Girls' Public Day School Company in 1873. Six years later Chelsea High School moved to Kensington, changing its name to Kensington High School, and there it prospered until 1941 when the building was destroyed by a land-mine. In 1948 it was reorganized as a Junior School, administered by the Girls' Public Day School Trust.

Notting Hill has also changed its locality, moving to Ealing from Norland Square, Notting Hill, in 1931. It is now known as Notting Hill and Ealing High School.

The Camden School was the second of the schools opened by Frances Mary Buss, and was established in 1871 in Camden Street when the original school moved to "more commodious premises."

St Martin's Middle Class School was originally another of the Charity Schools of Westminster, opened in 1700 by the Society for the Promotion of Christian Knowledge. After the Endowed Schools Act of 1869 it became a recognized secondary school, and in 1873 a scheme was approved by Her Majesty for the St Martin's Middle School for Girls. In 1894 the name was changed to the St Martin-in-the-Fields High School for Girls. In 1928 it moved out to Tulse Hill, to buildings provided by the London County Council and so became an aided school.

Manchester High School is an example of a school which rose "out of the needs of the community," the creation of a body of

Manchester citizens, men and women, none of whom was "an educational expert." The Manchester Association for Promoting the Higher Education of Women, in its Report for 1871, recommended "the foundation of a public day school for girls to the City of Manchester as a great want of the times," and by 1873 the organization of such a school was nearly completed. In the first school Report the Committee stated that the special and peculiar merit of the school lay "in the security offered by public Governors of the School and an independent and frank yearly Report of the School; and in the moderation of the terms on which such high education is offered . . . such a School for Girls has become manifestly a requirement of the times in all large towns . . . women's interests and education have hitherto not had justice and fair play, . . . such a school is a pressing need in this city in particular, and could still only scantily provide for Manchester's daughters what has been provided without stint for Manchester's sons."

So the first nine schools are of striking interest, an epitome of the schools that were shortly to be included in membership; but in spite of their divergencies there was no thought of forming separate associations. From early days Frances Mary Buss and Dorothea Beale worked together, and although their opinions frequently differed they shared their difficulties and compared their views, gradually drawing in others to enlarge the circle until the time came to form an association and the meeting in Myra Lodge was held.

The nine pioneers were quick workers and immediately sent invitations to the head mistresses of Plymouth High School, Keighley Grammar School, Croydon and Norwich High Schools, the Ladies' College, Guernsey, Huddersfield Girls' College and Liverpool Collegiate School, an indication of the rapid geographical spread of the Association. The minutes of the meeting were taken by Louisa Brough, a personal friend of Frances Mary Buss, who, being aware of the practical interest she had shown in the movement for girls' education, claimed her as a helper for the Association "in its infancy." She became the first secretary and when she retired in 1901 the Executive Committee recorded their gratitude for "the constant zeal and courtesy with which she had served the Association since its formation."

At the first Annual General Meeting, held in February 1876 at Camden Lodge, a balance sheet was presented which stated, "Receipts from subscriptions for the year 1875 amounted to £8.0s.0d. and the expenditure to £1.17s.6d., leaving a balance in hand of £6.2s.6d. Six pounds were presented to the Secretary for her services." It is uncertain at what date this "gratuity" became a regular remuneration, but in May 1887 "the secretary's salary was increased from fifteen to twenty guineas in view of the increased work of the Association." The first office was at 112 Brompton Road, London SW, but by 1887 it had been transferred to 17 Buckingham Street, Adelphi, London.

From 1877 annual conferences were held, deliberately arranged in different localities, and these were important occasions in the schools which acted as hostesses. During the first ten years they met in schools in Cheltenham, Bradford, Notting Hill, Plymouth, London, Manchester, Croydon, Clifton, Bristol and Oxford. Even in the 1870s railway travel was something of an adventure, and the organization of a conference no light matter, especially in the middle of a school term. The conferences have never been limited to representatives or delegates, but have been open to all members, gathered from all parts of the British Isles. Alice Morison, who joined the Association at the age of twenty eight, and became one of its leading speakers and a life member, left this personal anecdote: "In 1896 I was appointed head mistress of Truro High School and my head mistress was delighted. When I told her that my salary was to be £200 a year, she told me never to think of it as more than £195 and to spend the extra £5 in always attending the Conference of the Head Mistresses. It was splendid advice for I owe more than I can ever say to our Association. Miss Beale was at the first meeting I attended and I remember so well signing the register immediately after her entry:

Dorothea Beale, Cheltenham	999 pupils
Alice R. Morison, Truro	99 pupils."

Conversation at the assemblies was so animated that a rule was made: "No conversation shall be permitted in the Conference Hall during debate. A second room shall be provided in which conversation may go on during debates." At first, the officers may have been a little at sea about procedure, but soon there was a formal Constitution, Rules of Debate were clearly stated, and all was under firm control. At the first Conference Frances Mary Buss was formally elected President of the Association—obviously it could not have been anyone else—and she presided over its fortunes until her death in 1894, by which time she had at any rate set it firmly on its feet, looking in the direction which she hoped it would take. The President of the Annual Conference was to be elected from year to year.

By 1881 an Executive Committee had been formed and rules for membership drawn up; forty members attended the Conference that year, and decided that in future this annual event should be held as near as possible to the June half-term, a practice to which the Association has adhered with fierce tenacity. In 1893 a sub-committee was formed "to consider means of relieving the over-worked President"! In 1896 an Incorporation Sub-Committee was set up, and it was stated that in drawing up the Memorandum of Articles of the Association the object was to allow for the utmost freedom of development; the name was changed to omit "Endowed and Proprietary Schools" because it was considered that the time might come when "Endowed and Proprietary" would not include all kinds of Public Secondary Schools, and therefore "the conditions of membership have been very carefully stated in the Deed itself." This was a far-sighted policy, and the action taken was quite deliberate, emphasizing the desire of the founders to preserve one Association. It was a matter of principle which was to lead to far greater stress of mind than they could have foreseen. They were pioneers but not prophets, and could have had no inkling of what was to happen in 1902, and again in 1944. But the principle had been asserted "that there should be one Association" and, when the strain came, one association it remained.

If today a new Nine Worthies should meet to review the state of the Association, they would find the professional, not to mention the personal, diversity of the membership astonishing. It would include head mistresses of schools which may be County, Voluntary Controlled or Aided, Special Agreement, Direct Grant or Independent; the schools may be day or boarding, for girls only or co-educational; they may be selective or non-selective, grammar, secondary modern, technical, bilateral or comprehensive, and the age range of the pupils may cover the full gamut of the traditional secondary years of eleven to eighteen plus or they may cover sections thereof, the middle school, the junior and senior high schools or the sixth form college. Finally they would include schools overseas as well as those in the United Kingdom. The position now is that any head mistress of a public secondary school which is recognized as efficient by the Department of Education and Science is eligible for ordinary membership of the Association. Frances Mary Buss would have applauded; Dorothea Beale might have raised an eyebrow but could hardly have withheld approval.

The growth and development of the Association have been a true reflection of the types of girls' secondary schools, varying in the nature of their government, in their curriculum and in the ability and circumstances of their pupils, which have been established in the past one hundred years. The deliberate inclusion of such a wide range of schools is a distinctive feature of the Association. The result of this policy has not only been a great enrichment to the Association itself but has brought about an understanding between girls' schools which could have been achieved in no other way, a combination of unity and diversity which has been a benefit to the whole of girls' education.

Chapter 2

Schools and more schools

The history of the Association of Head Mistresses cannot be written without taking into account the wider background of events against which it is set, for it constantly reflects the social, economic and educational changes which have taken place in the last one hundred years. Sometimes the Association has been at the mercy of those events, sometimes it has played a part in shaping their outcome, but the story is one which can be understood only in its proper setting. It was, for instance, the impetus of the women's movement which made the pioneer schools so enterprising. The differences which have gradually come to distinguish girls' schools from boys', differences in ethos, curriculum and intention, are partly due to the fact that the girls' schools were making a fresh start, and "having no tradition either to guide or hamper them" were compelled to think out their creed *ab initio* in order to justify their very existence. This produced creative thinking, the birth of new ideas, and the modification or reform of practices which for many years no one had thought to question.

The contribution which head mistresses might be expected to make to the whole of education was recognized as early as 1887 by no less an educationist than Edward Thring, the headmaster of Uppingham, who invited the Association to a conference in his school. An account of this given in his *Life and Letters* reveals the curious state of the boys' public schools, impregnable in their strongholds, as well as the great encouragement and pleasure which his action gave to the head mistresses.

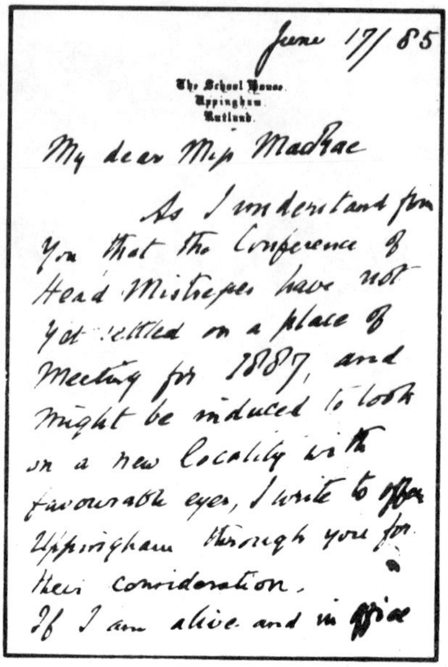
June 17/85

The School House.
Uppingham.
Rutland.

My dear Miss MacRae

As I understand from you that the Conference of Head Mistresses have not yet settled on a place of meeting for 1887, and might be induced to look on a new locality with favourable eyes, I write to offer Uppingham through you for their consideration.

If I am alive and in office

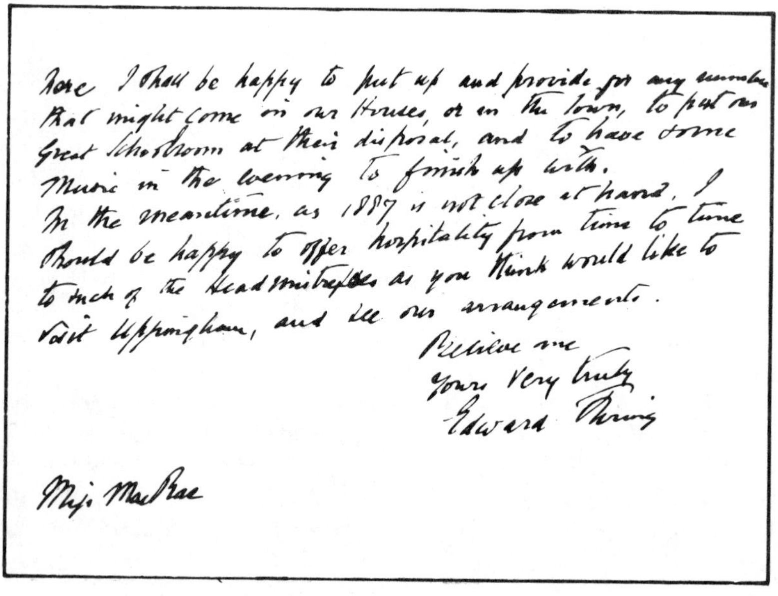
here I shall be happy to put up and provide for any number that might come in our Houses, or in the town, to put our Great Schoolroom at their disposal, and to have some Music in the evening to finish up with.

In the meantime, as 1887 is not close at hand, I should be happy to offer hospitality from time to time to such of the Head mistresses as you think would like to visit Uppingham, and see our arrangements.

Believe me
Yours very truly
Edward Thring

Miss MacRae

Edward Thring's invitation to meet at Uppingham.

In 1869 a conference of head masters had been held at Uppingham, which Thring felt "had given rise to much sympathetic and useful interchange of thought, and had broken down some of the ancient isolation of the greater schools. But in the intervening years new and powerful educational forces had come into play. Amongst the most interesting were those directed to the higher education of girls: the high schools and colleges were becoming a power in the land and the impulse was extending to the universities. The leaders of the movement had much indifference and prejudice to combat, but they had no ancient traditions to hinder them from recognizing the value of intercourse and co-operation."

In order to foster this co-operation, Edward Thring sent an invitation to the Association of Head Mistresses and on 10 June 1887 "the lady teachers of England" held their annual conference at Uppingham. To quote his own words, "It was a grand day. Fifty-nine actually came, and we did all in our power to honour them. We put them all up, fêted them, gave them a concert and in all ways entertained them as royally as we could. It was the first official recognition they had had, which made it the more important, and a greater pleasure to all parties. They were a delightful company, entirely free from all nonsense: not a trace of 'women's rights' amongst them, but most sensible, sober-minded workers and thinkers. . . . everything went off with the most splendid success and a very remarkable set of able and interesting women they were. . . ."

In his address to the Conference he said that if new thinking and necessary reforms were to be introduced in education it would be by women—"You are fresh, and enthusiastic, and comparatively untrammelled whilst we are weighed down by tradition, cast like iron in the rigid moulds of the past. . . . the hope of teaching lies in you."

The Uppingham masters and "the school ladies" shared in the conference and the whole occasion made such an impression on the head mistresses that Frances Mary Buss wrote afterwards on their behalf asking Dr Thring "to accept for your library a few books, in remembrance of our visit to Uppingham. It ought not to pass without leaving a token in your possession for it is an event in educational history of no small significance."

The phrase "an event in educational history of no small

significance" pulls one up short. Have Thring's high hopes been fulfilled? Has the Association made a significant contribution to education as a whole? This obviously is a theme which this book will pursue, but it is perhaps worth while to quote the Spens *Report on Secondary Education* published fifty years later in 1938. It says, "The new High Schools for Girls were to a great extent unfettered by the traditions and prejudices which obsessed the endowed schools for boys, and the new mistresses were more responsive to new ideas, more critical and more disposed to adapt themselves to changing circumstances." The early members of the Association needed courage in facing these "changing circumstances," for they were still feeling their way, each in her own sphere, with no common policy to guide them, and no common background of education against which to assess their experiences.

With regard to their academic credentials, very few of course held degrees. A number had attended courses at Queen's College, Bedford College, or the College of Preceptors, and at various centres in the North of England there were lectures and courses sponsored by the Association for Promoting the Education of Women, so that in one way or another those who took charge of the schools had secured certain certificates. These they cherished as representing their success in the face of opposition, and the extent to which they were prized is shown by the attitude of Frances Mary Buss herself. She had been made an Honorary Fellow of the College of Preceptors and requested that the letters F.C.P. should be inscribed after her name on her tombstone. But although these women had never had the chance of acquiring formal paper qualifications, they were by no means uneducated. They were often proficient in several languages which they had perfected by study abroad, well read in English literature, thoroughly familiar with the Bible, and probably interested in painting or music. Some had studied Latin and Greek with their fathers or brothers. They came mostly from the cultured homes of the professional classes, were accustomed to good conversation, reading aloud from the English classics, and providing their own amusements.

Many of them, in their memoirs, pay tribute to the value of the education they received from their parents, far outweighing that from any other source. This tradition of home life they brought to their schools, which in consequence retained something of the atmosphere of a large family. Frances Mary Buss is said to have distributed sweets when visiting the Juniors, and one reminiscence of her is that when she drove to school each morning in her four-wheeler she would stop when she passed North Londoners carrying heavy satchels and have these piled on the roof of the cab.

Ivy Browning, a former pupil of Cheltenham, recounted an incident which shows the personal attention that Dorothea Beale, unapproachable to many, gave to one child. She said, "At one of the weekly mark-readings for the middle school Miss Beale said to the form mistress, 'Ivy Browning shall come and read to me in the holidays.' The words fell on my ears like a death knell. I went, was handed *Lorna Doone* and could not make Miss Beale hear. So I said, 'Shall I fetch my sister, she learns elocution?' 'Yes,' she said, 'send Stella.' Stella got on famously, and to reward her daily efforts, Miss Beale gave her a dry biscuit."

Most of the head mistresses were in their early twenties, very young for the responsibilities they were carrying, and had led sheltered lives. Now they had not only to turn to practical problems, but in many cases had also to struggle against formidable odds. In the first place, the schools nearly always had to start in unsuitable premises, making do with whatever could be found: perhaps a pair of terrace houses joined together, a medley of dark stairs and landings and cold rooms, heated only by coal fires. Although the schools were termed "Endowed and Proprietary" the endowment was usually in name only and brought no material benefits. Girls' schools have always been dogged by lack of funds, and in those early days they suffered from actual poverty. The founders were so anxious to keep the fees moderate that they were often far too low, with the result that even essential equipment was lacking. Not all head mistresses had Frances Mary Buss's passion for experiment and her flair for discovering the latest models in desks or gymnastic apparatus; many of them were quite bewildered by suddenly having to order furniture and books on an unaccustomed scale. The Bryce Report on Lancashire Schools mentions the want of the most elementary equipment, "the absence of desks in which ink bottles can be fixed" and "the irregularity and slovenliness which is so frequent a fault in girls' schools." Head mistresses of endowed schools had been known to eke out the salaries of their assistants from their own pockets, and in one instance one of Her Majesty's Inspectors noted, "A Head Mistress receiving a legacy actually expended £700 on desks and apparatus, and this in a public endowed school."

Another difficulty was the complete absence of standard amongst the pupils entering the schools, some of them eighteen or nineteen years old. They flooded eagerly in, some having been taught at home, some with a smattering of French and Mathematics very inaccurately learnt, some with no pretence at anything but "accomplishments." Girls of fourteen or more might know less than some of the younger ones, but all had to be admitted and somehow sorted into teachable groups. Most of them had no idea of what was going to be demanded of them when once they had entered the school. They expected to stay just for a year or two, and to leave when they liked; the head mistress of Carlisle High School said in 1894, "It is almost an insult to high schools to treat them (as they do), to consider that they ever aimed at being in the nature of finishing schools. If they are anything they demand to train the girl throughout. . . ."

The most serious difficulty of all, however, was the lack of competent teachers, for although the recruits showed goodwill and enthusiasm there is no doubt that these frequently ran ahead of their abilities. Schools which were favourably placed could get assistance from qualified men, lecturers in colleges, canons of cathedrals and other well-disposed clergymen and professors. Very often the relatives of the head mistress or staff were pressed into service, but in many instances none of this help was available and there are records of very poor teaching, and the imparting of incorrect information. Emily Davies, giving evidence to the Taunton Commission, said, "Even the best women teachers complain that they have had very imperfect training and education themselves and are hampered by want of money," and Bryce, to quote him again, commented, "The teachers have not themselves been well taught and they do not know how to teach. Both these defects are accidental and may be remedied."

Remedied they were, and this more than anything else transformed the schools. From about 1860 onwards, pupils began to emerge from the pioneer high schools, and before long they were able to go straight on to higher education, for between the years 1869-1900 a succession of women's colleges was created and new developments took place in the universities. Hitchin (later Girton College) was founded in 1869; Merton Hall (to grow into Newnham College) in 1871; and in the same year Newcastle College of Science, which was open to men and women. In 1877 the Maria Grey Training College came into being and during the next few years Somerville, Lady Margaret Hall and St Hugh's College, Oxford, and Westfield and Royal Holloway Colleges in London. In 1880 the University of London admitted women to all its degrees, as did the Royal University of Ireland and Trinity College, Dublin. Others followed suit. The Victoria University (Liverpool, Manchester and Leeds), established between 1880 and 1887, was from the first open to both men and women. Oxford did not give degrees to women until 1921; Cambridge held out until 1948 before conceding full degrees. It was in 1873 that two Hitchin students were successful in the Cambridge Classical Tripos and one in the Mathematics Tripos, although they were unable to obtain degrees. Two of the staff of the North London Collegiate School were among the first women to be awarded degrees of the University of London in 1880, and in 1883 Bedford College rejoiced over its first Arts graduates. In 1884 Sophie Bryant, later the head mistress of the North London Collegiate School, made history by taking the final degree of Doctor of Science in the Moral Science branch, and was the first woman to be awarded a doctorate in the University of London. So, at last, the barriers were coming down, and, as the supply of qualified teachers holding degrees or the equivalent became available to the schools, the standard of teaching rapidly improved.

In 1891 Frances Mary Buss, reviewing the change in girls' schools during her lifetime, was able to say, "The vast improvement which has taken place during the last fifteen years has been brought about mainly by the improved education of their teachers," and again, "The composition of our Staff tends to become more and more marked by the presence of women with university attainments equal to those of men, but who are superior to the assistant masters in the possession of knowledge as to the principles underlying their work and the methods by which these principles can be applied," an interesting comment, indicating the difference between men and women in their attitude towards professional training.

The Friends' Schools had been pioneers in apprenticeship schemes for training, but in 1890 the head mistress of the Mount School, York, announced that she would "no longer need to rely on these, for she would in future appoint none but university graduates to the posts that fell vacant on the staff, and so bring the school into line with modern educational methods and outlook."

For many years, of course, the standard of staffing remained uneven, with unqualified women teaching in the schools as late as the 1930s, and it is impossible to generalize. The variety of schools in membership of the Association became more pronounced as the years went on, and one has to think of it in about 1880 as a medley of schools and standards. There were, for instance, a number of schools which had grown from charity foundations, each with a history which stretched back for a century or more before the Association even came into existence. Such schools were the Burlington School, Shepherds Bush; The Godolphin School, Salisbury (founded in 1726 for "six poor gentlewomen"); The Red Maids' School in Bristol, and the Mary Erskine School in Edinburgh (originally the Merchant Maiden Hospital), all founded specifically for girls. There were others, such as Christ's Hospital and the Grey Coat Hospital, founded to give boys and girls up to twelve years old an education suitable for their age and station in life. Many of these schools were in a bad way, but as a result of the Endowed Schools Act of 1869 new schemes were drawn up for their administration, and they were reorganized as separate schools for boys and girls at the secondary school level. This not only gave a great impetus to the movement for girls' secondary education but also resuscitated the schools, which were soon making considerable intellectual advance. They could not, however, immediately escape from their early regulations, traces of which long remained in the curriculum, the premises, and the uniform. Records give a picture of girls in expensive heavy cloth dresses (grey or red), pleated fore and aft, with a white piqué stomacher and white collar and cuffs, on a foundation of home-made stays, black serge petticoat and chemise. At the Grey Coat Hospital, Elsie Day (Madam, as she was always called), finding the clothes not only cumbersome but inadequate for any form of recreation, requested a bale of calico "to make drawers for the girls." "Why?" asked Baroness Burdett-Coutts, "I have never worn drawers." "No," was the reply, "but then your Ladyship does not go up in the swings." Madam got her calico. These schools had moved on from "reading, writing, a little arithmetic and a good deal of plain sewing," to a more intellectual curriculum and were all set to take part in the major movement in girls' education.

Then there were others with somewhat similar foundations but not quite in the same category, which under the Endowed Schools Act discovered that funds, hitherto used for boys alone, were available for girls, and so new schools for girls came into being. Such a school was Keighley Girls' Grammar School, stemming from the Free Grammar School founded for boys in 1739. In 1871 a scheme was issued by the Board of Education by which a Trust was formed to administer the Drake and Tonson's Girls' School (as it was called until 1934) "to supply a liberal and practical education for girls in the Parish of Keighley." It was to be in the charge of a governing body, four of whom were to be women, and it was to receive £250 per annum for the boys' endowment. It claims to be the first of its kind to be opened in England, and the first head mistress was Mary Eliza Porter. A similar foundation is Bradford Grammar School for Girls which is, strictly speaking, a branch of Bradford Boys' Grammar School, dating from 1662, but is administered by a separate scheme and has a separate governing body. Here again, it was to receive the sum of £250 per annum from the earlier foundation, but a sum of £5,000 was collected by friends of education in Bradford to purchase the building. In due course the governors appointed the first head mistress, none other than Mary Eliza Porter. An outstanding example of the use of endowments being diverted to found girls' schools is the King Edward VI Foundation in Birmingham, which is responsible for five girls' schools. When the first of these, the King Edward VI High School for Girls, was founded in New Street in 1881, the Boys' High School had to squeeze itself into closer quarters and in its turn encroach on the head master's home. The natural reaction of the staff of the boys' school was expressed in the remark of one much-tried master who "wished that all the girls of Birmingham had but one neck, and that had a rope around it."

Other famous schools which came into being in much the same way are the schools of the great London City Companies. Haberdashers' Aske's Acton School, whose origins are found in an almshouse and school for boys, was set up in Hoxton in the late seventeenth century. In 1875 girls were admitted, in 1900 the Hoxton school was closed as the site was considered undesirable, and the building in Acton was opened in that year. Another example is the Mary Datchelor School. This came into existence through the Datchelor Charity, but owes its prosperity to the generosity of the Clothworkers' Company, which has been responsible for it since 1894.

The readiness with which the proposals of the Endowed Schools Commission were adopted is a testimony to the growing public awareness of the poor state of education for girls, and the last part of the nineteenth century saw not only the transformation of existing schools but also the founding of new secondary schools for girls, in all parts of the country. Some of these were founded by private benefactors; some by groups of business men or generous-minded citizens, in London, Manchester, Liverpool, Birmingham, Bristol, Newcastle and many other towns. They were day-schools, the outcome of the wealth and prosperity of the cities, and to the cities they belonged. Some were promoted by men and women in cathedral cities or intellectual centres, a practical expression of religious belief and learning. Some were denominational, set up by Church Schools Companies or such bodies as the Quakers (though most of them were much earlier foundations), many of these being boarding schools. Others, like those of the Girls' Public Day School Company, were free of denominational ties. All over the British Isles girls' schools came to life, varying greatly in atmosphere, efficiency and wealth, but with the same common purpose, to further the education of girls of the middle and upper classes.

In 1871 an event took place which strengthened the hands of all those engaged in this movement. This was the formation of the "National Union for improving the education of women of all classes," the founder and chairman of which was Mrs William (Maria) Grey. There are amongst Frances Mary Buss's papers the annual reports of the Union for the years 1871 to 1874, and a preamble which states, "Reports of the Schools Inquiry Commission, published 1868-9, revealed a state of things as regards Girls' Schools and Female Teachers, calling urgently for large and active reform. Various associations to promote this reform were founded: the largest and most important was the North of England Council, followed somewhat later by the Yorkshire Board of Education. Educational Associations to establish lectures and classes for ladies sprang up in many places in the United Kingdom. Individuals and Associations were often working towards the same end in ignorance of each other's action, of what had been and of what remained to be done. There is no common centre for exchange of information." Maria Grey had the idea of setting up such a centre and enlisted the help of the Society of Arts in carrying it into execution. A central committee was formed, two members of which were James Bryce, and Frances Mary Buss who represented the London Schoolmistresses' Association. The secretary was Louisa Brough.

The Report for 1871 lists thirty-six counties, and in them the towns where branches of the Union had been formed; the list also includes Wales, Scotland and Ireland. Here are given in full the names of the members of each Branch and the result is a remarkable record, preserved almost by chance, of the men and women all over the country who had set themselves to provide a new kind of education for girls. Amongst them most of the girls' schools now in membership of the Association of Head Mistresses which were in existence at that time would find the names of their founders and supporters. Reference is made to lectures, classes and library facilities arranged for young women at Rugby, Windsor and Clifton, Bristol, where the masters from Rugby School, Eton and Bristol Grammar School "had given their time and skill most generously to the work." No doubt the Rugby classes were those mentioned by Elizabeth Day in her autobiography. The report ends with the words, "From this brief summary, imperfect as it is, it will be seen that new life is manifesting itself in many directions."

The National Union appointed several sub-committees, one of special interest being the "Sub-Committee for the Application of Endowments to Girls." This committee evidently worked closely with the Endowed Schools Commission, and each year it reported faithfully on the progress being made, the schemes which had been approved, and others not yet completed. It brings to life the work done by the Commission, and the tremendous encouragement given to girls' schools which suddenly found at their disposal funds beyond their wildest dreams.

Another object of the Union was the establishment of "good and cheap day schools for all classes above those attending the elementary schools," and these were the first schools of the Girls' Public Day School Company, now the Girls' Public Day School Trust.

While these influences were at work in the country, the Association of Head Mistresses was busy putting its house in order, and the records of the first ten or twenty years throw light on the subjects which were occupying the minds of members—some of them strangely familiar, though wearing a different guise.

Between the years 1874 and 1890 much thought was given to teacher training, though when the subject was first put before the Association it met with considerable opposition. Frances Mary Buss, however, had always been a staunch advocate of training and done everything in her power to secure training qualifications of some kind for all teachers, persuading the Home and Colonial Institute to arrange a course for secondary teachers, supporting the efforts of the College of Preceptors, and insisting that her own staff should obtain any certificate available. She was one of the Council of the Maria Grey Training College, founded in 1878 as the first college giving training for secondary school teaching, and both she and Sophie Bryant were closely connected with the Cambridge Training College (later Hughes Hall) founded in 1885. Teacher training was the subject of the Conference held at Cheltenham in 1877, resulting in a memorial being submitted to Oxford and Cambridge asking these universities to establish an examination for teachers and to extend it to London. Dorothea Beale believed in the idea of apprenticeship for teachers, and in 1885 a Secondary Training Department became a recognized section of Cheltenham Ladies' College. In 1888 the Datchelor Training College was opened by the Mary Datchelor School, Camberwell; Milton Mount College had a Training College attached and opened two other schools in Gravesend to provide teaching practice; and there were other examples up and down the country.

Two factors which led the Association to give strong support to the promotion of training were firstly the desperate need for more efficient teachers, and secondly the lack of any other qualification obtainable by women; for many years it was the only way of establishing any professional status. Schoolmasters, who held degrees, never took kindly to the idea, and as university courses became available for women they too were inclined to reject it. Sophie Bryant, speaking about the establishment of the Cambridge Training College, said, "We were much exercised by the fact that the women educated at the universities persisted in neglecting professional training. Either they despised it, or could not afford it, or could get entrance to the schools without it"; so the issue became bound up with the great contention which has only recently been resolved as to whether training is really necessary for the university graduate. Frances Mary Buss and Sophie Bryant both saw the danger of a split into two categories, for they asked whether "anything could be done to avert this growing danger that the teaching profession should fall into the two classes of those who were highly educated and not trained, and of those who were trained but not highly educated." It was to avoid this that the Cambridge Training College was begun. It was intended for women graduates, but it soon became apparent that these would be in a minority amongst the students. So the split occurred, not just between two types of secondary school teacher, but between the secondary and elementary sections. This was much more serious and was to have far-reaching repercussions, but it is doubtful whether, at the time, it could have been averted. It is one example of the way in which circumstances were too strong for the Association to achieve its real intentions.

Closely allied to the complications of qualification was the question of registration, again because of the effect it had on professional status. In 1879 the Association held a special

A PAGE FROM THE TIME-TABLE, 1875.

THURSDAY.

Form	VI	V	IV	III	II	I
8.30	French	Study	Zoology	Zoology	Piano	Scrip.
9.15	Study or Piano	Study or Piano	French	Arith.	Study	French
10	Piano	French	Arith.	Scrip.	Scrip.	Scrip.
WALK.						
12	Latin	Study	French	Piano	French	French
12.40	Arith.	Euclid	Euclid	Study	Reading	Study or Piano
1.20	Botany	Piano	Geography	Study	Study	French
2.45.	**NEEDLE-WORK AND WALK OR GARDEN.**					
4.20	Scrip.	Scrip.	Scrip.	E. Hist.	French	Grammar
4.55	Drawing	Drawing	Dictation	Drawing	Arith.	Geography
5.30	Drawing	Drawing	Arith.	Piano	E. Hist.	Drawing
6.30	Study	Study	Drawing	Drawing	Drawing	Play

Timetable from the Annals of Milton Mount College, compiled by Selina Hadland (1873-89). The long morning session was for many years a characteristic of girls' schools.

meeting to discuss and approve in principle the Bill for the Registration of Teachers, but also to object to the very small representation of women on the Educational Council proposed by the Bill. In 1894 there was a request to give evidence before the Bryce Commission, then dealing with the subject of a classified register.

Not only was the Association busy with training and registration but it was also concerned with the welfare of assistant staff, and exercised for many years over the establishment of a Provident or Pension Fund. At the first Annual General Meeting in 1876 a discussion took place on the desirability of forming a pension fund for assistant mistresses, and in 1879 the Charity Commissioners were petitioned by the Association to take into account in all their future schemes pensions for assistant masters and mistresses as well as for heads of schools. In 1894 a pensions scheme, similar to that of the Head Masters' Association, was drawn up by a sub-committee appointed for the purpose, and in 1898, owing to the joint efforts of the two associations, a pensions scheme for heads and assistants was secured through the Imperial Life Office. By 1898 the governing bodies were actively encouraging this arrangement.

Some of the time, however, was given to more domestic, and no doubt more congenial matters; School Hours, Examinations, Curriculum, Health, Prizes and Punishments and so on. For a long time there was considerable anxiety about health as no one knew how much pressure the emancipated female could stand, and co-operation was sought from parents with regard to suitable dress, early bed-times, fresh air and exercise. In 1880 the Association showed itself aware of wider obligations by sending a strong appeal to the National Health Society to establish playgrounds in London.

On public examination there were two schools of thought. Frances Mary Buss was strongly in favour, but Dorothea Beale objected to girls taking the same examination as boys, not only because the subjects were unsuitable, but more because the effects of rivalry might prevent a girl from wearing "the true ornament of a meek and quiet spirit."

The Association expressed its opinion on examination syllabuses and the iniquities of examiners, particularly those of the

Royal Academy of Music. Their results were alleged to be unreliable because there was no common standard, and a formal request was made that local teachers and secretaries should never be allowed to examine in their own areas. The Academy was also reprimanded for its readiness to grant certificates of ability to teach music to quite incompetent people—some, apparently, even unable to play an instrument. There is evidence of a dawning interest in international affairs, for in 1880 Frances Mary Buss urged members to attend the Brussels Educational Conference, and in 1893 Sara Burstall (Manchester High School) represented the Association at the Chicago Exhibition. In 1886 an appeal for sympathy and help came from the Indian schools and five pounds was voted for the funds, and in 1879 a report was received from the head mistress of the High School in Mussoorie, entitled "First Impressions of Indian Education in Secondary Schools," showing that a link had been formed. Through these years certain ideas on girls' education were taking shape and head mistresses were beginning to assert their opinions, both as individuals and as a body.

1887 was the year of the Queen's Jubilee, and the Association saw fit to send her a loyal address. A draft of this (drawn up by the ever-ready Eliza Porter) was considered at the May Executive, the sum of five guineas was approved to have it "engrossed," and it read as follows:

Address to the Queen on her Jubilee

May it please your Majesty

We, your Majesty's faithful subjects, members of the Association of Head Mistresses of Endowed and Proprietary Schools for girls in England, desire to offer you our loyal and hearty congratulations on the attainment of this the Jubilee of your Majesty's reign.

In doing this we are forcibly reminded of the remarkable change, amounting to a revolution which has taken place during the latter part of your Majesty's reign in the conditions and prospects of the education of women. . . .

The opportunity for gaining sound and accurate knowledge and the pleasure arising from cultivated tastes which now, through the establishment of the Higher Public Schools for girls in every large town in England, the opening of University Examinations to girls and women, the raising of the standard of education through the foundation of Colleges for Women like Girton and Newnham and the training of women for the work of Teaching—through these and other means the boon of sound education and thorough mental training has been placed within the reach of the great mass of Englishwomen.

We humbly offer to your Gracious Majesty our best wishes and hearty prayers for your continued happiness and prosperity, both as a sovereign reigning over a loyal people and as a mother surrounded by the love and devotion of her children.

Trusting that your Majesty may long be spared to reign over us. We have the honour to be your Majesty's loyal and obedient subjects.

It was as well that the Association had not seen the Queen's letter to the Princess Royal in which she had expressed her conviction that "education can be *overdone*."

Association of Head Mistresses
Of Endowed and Proprietary Schools,
112, BROMPTON ROAD, S.W.

The Annual Conference will be held on Friday, March 1st, and Saturday March 2nd, at the Girls' Grammar School, Bradford.

Agenda
Friday. March 1.

2.30 Dinner
3.30 Opening of Conference
  1. Routine business
  2. Paper to be read by Miss Porter on "The Course of Study in Girls' High Schools" to be followed by a discussion.
  3. Special questions to be discussed:
    (a) The difficulties connected with the arrangement of home work, for pupils in higher forms.
    (b) The arrangement of a curriculum so as to secure width & thoroughness without over work.
    (c) The arrangement of the curriculum

in reference to the value of the subject in itself, and its educational value.

Saturday March 2 1878

10 a.m. Discussion of questions suggested by members of the Association the subjects of which should be sent to the Secretary not later than Feb. 20th

2.p.m. Dinner

You are requested to inform Miss Porter, Girls' Grammar School, Bradford before Feb. 20th, whether you will, or will not be able to attend. Miss Porter will be happy to show the Grammar School, on Friday morning, to those ladies who can arrange to reach Bradford, on Thursday Evening In writing to Miss Porter, please state if you will arrive on Thursday evening or Friday morning
Louisa Brough
Secretary

Agenda for an early conference 1878. Written in longhand by the secretary, Louisa Brough, and duplicated by means of hectograph ink and "a jelly." In 1891 she was "authorized to purchase a cyclostyle for printing agenda."

Chapter 3

"By no means tame or tameable"

Gradually the prestige and influence of the Association grew, and it was consulted on an increasing number of educational topics. Meanwhile what was happening within the schools? Here, too, order was emerging and a pattern, though not one of deadly uniformity, was becoming established. Although the Association is primarily an "Association of Head Mistresses," it has always thought of "schools in membership," as well as head mistresses, partly because in the early days the schools were so closely identified with their heads that it was almost impossible to think of one without the other. Even though that phase has passed the Association still feels a professional concern for the welfare of a school as well as for that of its head mistress, and is always ready with help and advice, not taking the line of "our member, right or wrong" but trying to find a solution which will be the right one for the school, as well as for the head mistress.

The establishment of recognized standards in the schools was greatly assisted by the emergence of the new type of teachers, professional women who had experienced the emancipation of university life and proved their abilities. They were sure of themselves and nearly always better qualified than the heads with whom they worked. It was the assistants who brought more professional standards and skills into the schools, but it was from the heads that they caught the inspiration of pioneers.

What were the characteristics of the schools at that time?

First, they were very much alive. Both heads and staff felt themselves to be part of a great movement and gloried in the fact that their talents were now in demand and could be used to the full. Many years later Lucy Savill (Lincoln High School) wrote, "the first Heads were mostly people of strong spiritual conviction, impelling them to serve their generation, but by no means tame or tameable. . . . buildings and equipment were often poor but such was the zest of the Head and her colleagues that no one noticed what was not there—it was far too stirring a business to know yourself part of a thing so young, so full of life."

Another feature was their individuality. There was no set pattern which the founders had to follow, no regulations imposed by an Authority, for they were "endowed and proprietary schools" and there was no regimentation. To quote Lucy Savill again, "The Girls' Public Schools of this country began by being as different as flowers in a garden, for they were the expression of the personality of their first Heads, all women of culture and intellectual power." This was true. The schools of the pioneers were pre-eminently *their* schools, their own creation, and the history of the school is part of the life-history of the founder, reflecting her character.

Even when a school was under the control of a governing body it retained a character of its own, and in most instances was allowed a remarkable degree of freedom in its development. It was the governors who had chosen the head mistress, presumably because they considered her the right person for that particular establishment and having appointed her they left the internal management and direction of the school in her hands; though in many instances they took a great personal interest in all that went on, and minutes of governors' meetings reflect the pride and concern they felt in its progress. The records of Manchester High School give a vivid account of its foundation, showing that the founders experienced much the same hopes and fears as the pioneer head mistresses and shared the responsibilities of the school's early years.

On 19 January 1874 the doors were opened for the enrolment of pupils. The school secretary, with two of the lady members of the committee, attended to receive the fees in person. Their excitement grew as the girls streamed in and the cash mounted up, and at the end of the day they "had to get a cab to take to the bank the heavy weight of gold that had been brought as fees"—piles of golden sovereigns! The committee felt themselves to be part of the school, and a former member of staff recalls that one of the governors had a very good library. "This he opened freely to all the mistresses with the one condition that borrowed books must be returned. . . . life was made much brighter and more interesting to members of the staff in the early days by the charming kindness and hospitality shown to them by different members of the governing body."

This freedom and variety have been greatly prized and are privileges which the Association has refused to surrender, battling for their preservation on more than one occasion. The outstanding personality of many of the early head mistresses helped to establish the tradition.

The Mount School, York, for instance, had, as one of its most famous head mistresses, Lydia Rous, a woman of "impelling force and quick sagacious mind . . . a three-dimensioned woman" of remarkable qualities. She encouraged the study of advanced mathematics and Latin, and to the end of her life was herself a student, so that her pupils, as one of them has written, "drank from a running brook and not a standing pool." Some girls were completely overawed by her, as she was not easy to approach, and "being frugal of speech she could create about her a conversational desert. Indeed, an American supper visitor supposed the Staff were not permitted to talk." Intimidating though she was, in later years her pupils realized how her influence had permeated the whole school. They remembered her wonderful readings of poetry, her surprising acts of personal kindness showing her knowledge of individual needs, and the Christian view of life as service which, through her, they had unconsciously absorbed.

A different personality was that of Alice Ottley, chosen by the governors as the first head mistress of the school which now bears her name. She was a woman of piety and charm, the eldest daughter of a vicar and accustomed from girlhood to carrying out duties in the home and parish. She had a cultivated mind, spoke three foreign languages, and although of a gentle disposition was adamant in her ideas on self-discipline and the service of others. Prayer was at the heart of her own living and was the mainspring of the life of the school, and she looked upon teaching as a definite vocation. In the school the discipline was strict, but "every individual felt that she had been taken into the life of the school, with its happy, busy, quiet order."

Former pupils writing for school chronicles remark in a surprising number of instances upon the frugal and simple personal tastes of the head mistress compared with the generous hospitality she offered to visitors, especially to Old Girls. They were always sure of a kindly welcome, and attention was given to every detail for their comfort.

Individuality was the more easily preserved because the schools were for the most part small, and the management of them very personal. They started with just a handful of pupils, anything from ten to forty, and only a few girls in each form, but they grew quickly, often reaching the 200 mark in a year or two. Many of the boarding schools remained at about this figure, and the day schools, even though they grew to three or four hundred, were still establishments of only moderate size, and retained many customs which dated from their foundation.

The head mistress herself did a great deal of teaching and certainly knew personally every pupil and something of her home background. There are many anecdotes revealing the kindness and perspicacity of the head and, even more important, the sympathy and understanding with which the head mistress helped any pupil in trouble. Many women work most happily through personal contacts, and this direct influence and personal concern of the head mistress became a tradition which has not wholly disappeared, even in the much larger schools of the present time.

In the boarding schools, particularly, their responsibilities and duties were very heavy. In the annals of Walthamstow Hall a former pupil, writing of Kate Unwin, the head mistress, says, "Only those who lived in the house with her can understand how full her life was. In addition to the great work of training the girls, she superintended the whole of the teaching, taking many subjects herself, from the lowest to the highest forms. Every detail of household management, all the arrangements in the garden, the poultry-yard, etc., were under her immediate direction, and she found time also to supervise the plain and fancy needlework in which she so much excelled. She was of course responsible for the choice of books, methods of teaching, arrangement of classes, school hours and holidays and the whole internal organization, management and discipline of the school. Her care of her pets will be recollected by all, and as long as we live we shall remember hearing her voice calling her Persian cats to bed, in tones loud enough to be heard in all the dormitories, long after we were supposed to be asleep." It is no wonder that with this tradition behind them, some head mistresses have found it difficult to master the art of delegation.

In day schools it was quite usual for the head mistress personally to supervise the dinner, of course for much smaller numbers than now, to make sure that the food "though plain, was nourishing and good." She was expected to identify herself with every department of the school's life. The buying of furniture, lighting and heating of the buildings and all such matters were her responsibility, for school Bursars were unheard of, and there was no one else to whom these things could be entrusted.

Some of these head mistresses were stern in appearance, and inspired a good deal of awe, but they understood the needs of children and young people. They encouraged the girls to produce simple plays and concerts, to amuse themselves by dressing up, and dancing, and to own small gardens. In the boarding schools the head mistress sometimes took personal charge of the recreation period, joining in the fun, and one ex-pupil of a boarding school recalls the alarming experience of galloping round the play-room with her head mistress, taking a vigorous part in the old singing game, "There was a jolly miller." Picnics, walks and rambles were common, and no chance was lost of having a long day's outing. The school birthday (or the head mistress's) could be celebrated in this way and schools with a church foundation had a holiday for Ascension Day and other festivals.

Reading played a great part in school life, a habit many head mistresses had acquired in their own childhood. Former pupils of many different schools speak of the lasting pleasure and benefit they derived from the quiet hours when the head mistress read aloud to them, sometimes poetry, sometimes a story. In one school the head mistress held weekly meetings for her staff at which, after necessary discussions on school questions, they sewed while the head mistress read to them! In day schools, too, time was often found for this reading aloud, either in special periods during the week, or such times as the last week of the summer term when, examinations being over, there was a feeling of respite and leisure.

The girls were also strongly encouraged to read for themselves, and one writer mentions that "It was *the thing* to read. . . . locust-like societies had not begun their devouring onslaught on chunks of time. . . . the girls enjoyed stretches of leisure surpassing the best dreams of to-day. . . . and bunches of girls, thrown back on their own resources, read steadily." The choice of reading matter was controlled by the head mistress, some being more enlightened than others. A scarcely credible incident recorded in the year 1889 is that a group of young teachers had settled down to what was to be a delightful afternoon with *Jane Eyre* when the head mistress appeared on the scene, and seeing the title of the book objected to their reading it until they were twenty-five. One wonders why they should be immune from contamination at that particular age.

The teachers concerned in this incident may have been young apprentices, but it illustrates the attitude of the staff in the early schools, and the extraordinary restrictions to which they submitted. In some schools the staff were required to live in the head mistress's house, or in prescribed lodgings, or at any rate within a certain radius from the school. The conditions in the lodgings might be Spartan in the extreme, the gas turned off at the main at 10 p.m. and only a candle left for use on the hall-stand. Of course there was no heating in the bed-sitting rooms and sometimes not even a stone hot-water bottle in the bed. As late as 1917 an assistant in one school was reprimanded by the head because her landlady had complained of her smoking in her rooms, and in 1925 another, in her fifth year of teaching, consulted her head mistress before she "shingled" her hair; in the same school the staff were forbidden to wear sleeveless frocks. Many stories are told of the advent of the bicycle, which was regarded at that time as the height of emancipation. In the 1880s a member of the staff of the Swansea High School was dismissed for riding down a respectable suburban street in "bloomers." In 1895, however, the first head mistress of Cardiff High School taught the first head girl to ride a bicycle in the school playground and the following year Mabel Annie Vivian, the newly appointed head mistress at Newport, asked the governors if she might ride a bicycle in the town; the request was refused because it might create a bad impression. However, a woman member of the governors volunteered to learn to ride so that she might accompany Mabel Annie Vivian, and this was allowed. At Carlisle High School the Art mistress, at a staff meeting, asked for permission to bring her bicycle to school, but it was agreed that a woman cyclist was very conspicuous and it would be better to wait until that form of exercise for women was more general. These examples of the control exercised by the head mistress over her staff show the constant anxiety that prevailed lest any action should damage the reputation of the school. It shows, too, a sense of responsibility for the younger members of her staff. The professional woman was still an object of suspicion and there was always the fear of offending against the Victorian code of respectability by "being conspicuous." Teachers, for their part, were afraid of losing their posts and were too uncomplaining. Salaries were low but those of the head mistresses were not much better; they expected little for themselves and treated their assistants in the same way. Many of the boarding schools, particularly those maintained by the Church, depended on the unstinting service given to them by heads and assistant staff.

In order to appreciate this attitude one has to understand the spirit which animated it and see it as one facet of the moral outlook of the mid-Victorian era, and the effect this had on every side of life. Some schools were denominational; others, though not sectarian, were motivated by Christian principles. In that age, it was unthinkable to divorce education from religion. When the Association was founded the educational trinity of Home, School and Church had not ceased to function, and for the pioneers there was no problem. The day started with School Prayers (not designated "Assembly") and pupils in many different establishments listened daily to the text, "Whatsoever thy hand findeth to do, do it with thy might that God in all things may be glorified."

In their Commemoration Services a number of schools, even

those that were secular in foundation, adopted a form of Bidding Prayer and prayed that "in all places set apart for God's honour and service, true religion and sound learning may forever flourish." Some schools compiled their own Prayer Book or Hymn Book which eventually formed a common bond between several schools, as newly-appointed head mistresses took the volume to their new schools, where it was soon adopted. Divinity or Scripture was a privileged subject, not relegated to an unpopular corner of the timetable but probably taught by the head mistress, assisted by a few carefully chosen colleagues. Even if a head mistress was not an orthodox believer and did not teach the subject herself, she made sure that it received due attention.

However, the most abiding influence came from the sense of vocation which many women brought to the profession of teaching. They took up the work not only as a means of livelihood but also as a way of serving their generation. Service was a keyword in the schools. Hence the Charities, of one sort or another, which nearly every girls' school supported. Hence the willingness on the part of the staff to work long hours, to undertake troublesome residential duties, and to find satisfaction in such tasks. Self-discipline was necessary to the service of others, and they believed that the best way of teaching their pupils this truth was by example. Hence, also, that concern for the needs of the individual which was to be a hallmark of the girls' schools, and to show itself in a variety of educational experiments. The secondary schoolmistress of that day had the same professional spirit as many head mistresses—a "belief in a liberal education in school, and preparation for service to the community when schooldays were ended."

Heads, as well as assistants, sometimes suffered from over-earnestness and a mistaken sense of their duties. One contrived to make her presence so all-pervading as to make the school believe that ". . . sitting at her table or standing in her doorway she had complete command of Form VI, the dining-room, the French room, the Mistresses' room, the staircase to the whole of the upper floors, the dressing room staircase, the varied life of the big hall, the entrance hall, the front door and pupils' entrance"! Life must at times have been intolerable for her staff and pupils as well as for herself.

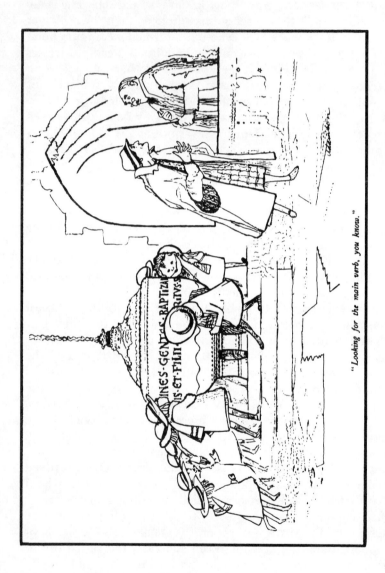

"Looking for the main verb, you know."

The image of over-earnestness in girls' schools persisted long after it had ceased to be a marked characteristic. (*By permission of Punch*)

In another school, a boarding school, the Saturday mornings were taken up with an established ritual. Each form in turn brought its exercise books, tied up in neat bundles, and laid them in piles on an office table. The head mistress then went methodically through the piles, assisted by the appropriate form mistress, and during the following week the whole school was assembled and each form in turn listened to a public exposure of its merits and deficiencies.

Undue emphasis was frequently laid on mark-readings, form order, percentages and the like, but it was by these methods that the head kept her finger on the progress of each individual, and set a standard where none had previously existed. It was for the staff as well as girls that a recognized standard was necessary, and though valuable time was taken up by the making of lists, meticulous corrections, and complex devices to encourage thoroughness and order, these demands were not considered unreasonable. A conscientious head mistress was concerned to eliminate slovenliness and slipshod work; petty restraints, endless supervision, over-attention to detail, all these were seen as the means to an end, a striving after excellence which stemmed as much from the religious basis of her professional ideas as from a scholar's passion for accuracy and perfection.

A publication of 1889, entitled *Work and Play in Girls' Schools*, by D. Beale, L. Soulsby and F. Dove, sets out precepts for teachers and parents. Some of them are surprisingly up-to-date, but running through the academic recommendations there is a strong vein of moral uplift which is characteristic of much of the thinking of that day. In the sections on music, for instance, there are excellent suggestions for the establishment of orchestras and choral classes, but a reason for this is "to counteract what is low and base and cultivate all that is true and fine and lovely." Art galleries are to be visited because of "the educative power of great paintings, by the study of which the pupil will come to understand higher teachings." Parents are told that "children should be allowed to put their home duties, but never their pleasure, before school. No leave of absence should ever be allowed for pleasure only, but where duty is involved, their attendance may be excused." Emphasis is constantly laid on the need to resist temptations, "Let us give to girls an invigorating dietary: physical, intellectual, moral. . . one cannot isolate the young, but they can be fortified." One chapter ends with the somewhat unfortunate rhyme:

> 'Tis life, not death, for which we pant,
> More life and fuller that we want.

Although these views were gradually modified, they persisted for a long time; their echo is found in such slogans as "Work for work's sake," reiterated in many girls' schools, and in the attitude which rejected prizes or any kind of rewards. It is found, too, in the rather pious mottoes and the symbolic flowers adopted by many schools as emblems. It was this self-conscious approach which helped to create the image of the over-earnest schoolmistress and the priggish schoolgirl, easily and frequently caricatured. Many teachers had enough humour to see this for themselves, and were fully aware of the impression popularly held. The Studies Committee of the Fabian Women's Group, investigating professional careers for women in 1914, stated that "the true teacher must have a vocation, but this earnest purpose should not destroy the woman teacher's sense of humour and of proportion. It is possible to take oneself and one's work too seriously."

Some of these characteristics were due to the fact that the movement was still feeling its way. Everything was new. Heads and assistants had to attain professional competence, and the Association as a whole had to acquire confidence in itself and win public support for its ideas. Gradually its members came to grips with fundamental educational problems and for the first time there emerged a body of women qualified to examine education from a professional standpoint, and to make known their views through a professional association. When the Education Act of 1902 was passed, there was already developing in the existing girls' schools an ethos which influenced the new ones coming into being. There was also an Association growing in numbers and strength, recognized as a professional body and ready to face the implications of the Act and to offer its considered opinion on how to meet the new situation.

Chapter 4

"A social revolution of the first magnitude" [1]

The turn of the century was a time of transition in society as a whole. The nineteenth century had laid stress on individual endeavour and voluntary effort in effecting social reform, but for the twentieth century this was not enough. Would-be reformers saw the need for well-directed organization and government aid if anything of significance was to be achieved, and this policy was soon to become apparent in education.

The provision of education for girls of the middle class had been in itself a revolutionary concept for many people; it was a vital stage in an educational revolution which is still continuing. The next stage came with the Act of 1902 aimed at the provision of secondary education by local authorities, and with it came the first major crisis in the Association's history.

At the end of the nineteenth century and beginning of the twentieth there was a marked increase in demands for better provision of schools by the state; much of it came from statesmen, educationists and leaders of industry. This was to be repeated in the years between the two world wars, reaching a climax in the preliminaries of the 1944 Act. Much of it also came from the general public, and it was the result of the undoubted success—in spite of all its obvious shortcomings and inadequacies—of the system of elementary education based on the 1870 Act. These forces together made a strong body of

---

[1] *History of the English People in the Nineteenth Century,* by E. Halevy.

Table I

Comparison of Cost of Education, and specially of Teaching per head, in the Elementary Schools, London, and in the Girls' Public Day Schools.

	Total Cost	Salaries including extras & head mistress		Salaries excluding extras		Salaries of assistants		No: of pupils per assistant teacher	No: of pupils per trained teacher
		Sum per head	Per cent of total cost	Sum per head	Per cent of total cost	Sum per head	Per cent of total cost		
A) Elementary School	£2.15.0	£2.0.10	74			£1.6.6	48	41	60
B) Girls' Public Day School	£13.4.10	£10.8.4	78	£8.16.9	66	£6.16.9	576	13	12.2
Ratio of A to B.	4.81	5.1		4.93		5.16		5.46	4.93

Costs of Education. A table compiled in 1893 during an investigation by the Association into the "inadequate and widely varying salaries of assistant mistresses." It illustrates with startling clarity some of the inequalities between elementary and secondary schools.

opinion although there were deep sectarian divisions among them. Even in 1902 there were still individuals so reactionary that their views coincided with those of the Duke of Wellington sixty years earlier when he had remarked to the Queen, "I don't know, Ma'am, why they make all this fuss about education." Others thought differently. Some were alarmed by the increasing commercial and industrial competition from countries like Germany and America, and the effect this would have on the nation's prosperity, and they could point to the greater spread and efficiency of state education in those countries. To quote the Rector of the University of St Andrews, "It is not too much to say that commercial and trade decay lies before us unless we can pull ourselves together in this matter. Where our competitors are spending thousands of pounds, we spend half a dozen pence." In one of a series of reports written for the Board of Education between 1895 and 1902 Michael Sadler expounded the novel belief that the existence of the British Empire depended not only on "sea power," which was a familiar and accepted idea, but rather on "school power," Experience in the Boer War had revealed very serious gaps and shortcomings in the education of the armed services at all levels. Charles Trevelyan, MP for Elland, had these dangers in mind when he spoke in the Commons debate. "This Bill," he said, "is demanded by the people from a sense of shame at our possessing the worst instructed peasantry in Western Europe, and fear on the part of our industrial population that we shall not be able to meet commercial competition." His use of the word "peasantry" has an oddly feudal ring about it; but he redeemed himself by giving as the third reason for the Bill the entirely modern belief "that the time has come when equality of opportunity should really be given to all men." This was the thinking of many national leaders. It was backed up by the significant fact that in 1900 there were 500,000 pupils in the elementary schools whose parents actually did not want them to leave at the age of twelve. These were to form the nucleus of the future secondary schools. It was against this background of national and political concern that the educational world, and of course the Association, started upon the challenging and controversial tasks that were to follow the passing of the Education Act of 1902. What had been achieved by the Association in the first thirty years of its history was the provision of educational opportunity for girls of the upper and middle classes. What was now to come was the extension of such opportunity to a far wider range of society, for the "deprived" were no longer the children of the well-to-do and the comfortably-off but the children—for the Association particularly the girls—of sufficient ability but insufficient means.

The Bill, soon to become the Education Act of 1902, began its long and arduous passage through Parliament to the accompaniment of great public interest. The debate in the Commons lasted for fifty-three days during which H.H. Asquith wearily remarked that the point had been reached when "it would be impossible for the wit of man to contribute any new idea to this discussion." Outside, the debate was continued on many platforms, and in 1901 and 1902 its provisions were the main theme for discussion at the conference and committee meetings of the Association of Head Mistresses. The sense of urgency "in view of imminent legislation" was strong. So was the sense of progress being made; and so were certain doubts. If secondary schools were to be set up by every local authority, would the status, the prestige, even the very existence of older schools be at risk? Would the cherished individuality of such schools be threatened if they were supported by the authorities? Would the teaching profession have a diminished part in guiding the course of education? Above all would the new Act prove to be a Trojan horse, bringing servitude in the guise of a gift? All these questions were asked, all these anxieties expressed in the Association. And in the minds of some head mistresses there hovered the unspoken, perhaps the almost unconscious, question whether the implied enlargement of their numbers might damage a tradition which over the last thirty years they had striven so hard to establish. Fifty had once been thought too large; would still greater numbers mean an inevitable loss of quality?

The crisis of thinking was real and it was honestly faced and dealt with. At the annual conference in 1901 the Bill was welcomed as requiring local authorities to provide "education other than elementary," with the caveat that in making this provision "the proposed authorities should have regard to the existing schools." In the following year, just before the Bill became law, the Conference again registered general approval, expressing however some sharp criticism, not of its liberal nature but of its failure to provide for the inclusion of women in the proposed Education Committees. This last point had been strongly made by Richard Jebb, MP for Cambridge, when he stated in the House, "It is said that women, who have been such valuable members of School Boards, will be excluded from Education Committees. Why on earth should they be excluded? . . . For my part I hold very strongly that women should have a place on *all* Education Committees." The general approval of the Association was, in fact, counterbalanced by many individual reservations. Edith Creak (King Edward VI High School, Birmingham) proposed a rider to the resolution of approval "thankfully recognizing the wisdom of the Government in not constituting one authority for secondary and elementary education." This was lost, but it was evidence of a not uncommon attitude, the tendency to think of elementary pupils (and their teachers) as a different and lesser breed, a tendency which has persisted for a long time, and not only among head mistresses.

Certainly a new era opened in 1902 with the passing of the Act, which achieved a great extension of educational opportunity. What it did not achieve was any union between elementary and secondary education, which were still regarded as fundamentally different in nature. Many of the pupils in the elementary schools remained there either because their parents could not or would not afford the modest fees charged by the new secondary schools (usually about one to three guineas a term) or because they were not successful in the competition for the limited number of free scholarship places. This divisive feature of the Act was masked by its generally progressive character, but there had been many head mistresses—Frances Mary Buss was one—who urged the importance of a link with elementary education and would have welcomed it had legislation made it possible. When it did not, they set to work within the framework they were given.

Legislation was followed by action. Although, as one might expect, some local education authorities were slow to move, the new secondary schools came into being at an ever-increasing rate. A large number of these were entirely new, some of them

Term one. 1906. Head Mistress
Beatrice Harriss K.A.T.E.?

The School began on Sept 13th 1906
with a roll call of 353 pupils.
111 of whom were pupils in the late
Endowed School for Girls. 199. from the
Higher Elementary. and the rest 43 new
pupils.
They were arranged in the following
Classes   16 in all
In the 4 years Scheme.

4th year   Form VI.   11.
3rd year   "   V. a. 27. V. b. . 23.
2nd year   "   IV. a. 30. IV. b. 28 IV. c 30.
1st year.   "   III a. 23 III. b. upper. 34.
Below the Course.
          III. a. lower. 14   III b. lower 32
          II. a. upper 21 II. b upper. 28
          II. a lower II. b. lower 18
          I. a. 15 I. b. . 7.

The majority of the classes were in the
School premises in Bolton Lane
but Forms III. b. lower & II. b. upper were
in two rooms in the Foundation St

The first entry (1906) in the records of Ipswich Municipal Secondary School for Girls, later Northgate School, showing how an old endowed school, the "higher top" of an elementary school and a number of new girls were brought together to form a secondary school.
(By permission of the County Borough of Ipswich Education Department)

being mixed schools under the control of a head master but many of them single-sex. As well as these, a great variety of established schools, some of them in difficulties, were transferred to local authorities and given a new lease of life.

Typical of schools taken over completely by the local authority was Allerton High School, Leeds. In 1900 Allerton, then a little village on the outskirts of Leeds, had no school accessible for young children, so in 1901 Helena Powell, head mistress of Leeds Girls' High School and a member of the Association, opened a small junior branch of the High School in Allerton. When her successor decided to close this, the parents formed a Limited Company and in 1905 opened an independent school, which flourished to such an extent that it became too big a concern for a private venture. In 1914 the school was transferred to the Leeds City Council, and by 1929 it occupied a whole terrace of houses and was a thriving establishment.

Similarly Falmouth County School began about 1887 as a private High School for Girls, with a kindergarten, run by a Limited Company with fifty-six shareholders and seventeen pupils. By 1908 there were over eighty pupils but this was apparently too much for the shareholders and the Company went into liquidation. The school was bought by the County Council who combined it with a Pupil-Teacher Centre to form a new school. Seven pupils were admitted as the first to hold "free places."

This mention of a Pupil-Teacher centre leads to yet another origin of the "new" schools. The Pupil-Teacher Centres were established in the last decades of the nineteenth century to cater for the continued education of those fourteen-year-olds who proceeded from the elementary schools, to become at first pupil-teachers and then to go to a training college or continue as uncertificated teachers in the elementary schools. Some of these centres formed the main starting point for the new County Schools; some, as at Falmouth, were combined with private schools, and although this was not an easy combination in one school, most of them proved a great success. Many County Schools, in all parts of the country, began with a nucleus of pupil-teachers among their first pupils.

Then there were the Higher Grade Elementary Schools for

the continued education of elementary school pupils. These were the schools which were regarded with such suspicion by Robert Morant, permanent secretary to the Board of Education, when he drew up the Regulations for Secondary Schools in 1904. The City of Bradford Education Committee was a pioneer in the establishment of these schools, and in 1902 a number of them, already flourishing, were promoted to the grade of High Schools by the local authority. Much hard feeling then and later would have been avoided had other authorities

NORTHGATE SCHOOL
FOR GIRLS, IPSWICH

This School, formerly known as the Municipal Secondary School for Girls, was founded in 1906 by the amalgamation of the Endowed Middle School for Girls [opened in 1886] and the Higher Grade School [opened in 1892]. It inherits, through the Endowed School for Girls, an ancient endowment existing in part in 1482.

The School moved from Bolton Lane to these buildings in September 1931.

LABOR OMNIA VINCIT

Northgate School, Ipswich: Commemorative Plaque
(By permission of the County Borough of Ipswich Education Department)

been as progressive, for the majority of these schools remained outside the new secondary sector.

As these schools became established, others, still financed and administered by voluntary bodies, began to find difficulty in meeting the expense of rising standards of buildings and equipment. Many of them were already in receipt of limited grants from public funds, but the 1902 Act empowered local authorities to come to their aid with grants in return for which the schools had to admit a given number of children from the elementary schools. This was the beginning of arrangements which incorporated these schools into the local provision for education and which led in 1944 to the status of voluntary aided and controlled schools. Such a school was the Orme Girls' School at Newcastle-under-Lyme in Staffordshire, which had started in 1876 when various educational endowments amalgamated. In 1906 the Borough came to its aid; it was already then a school of three hundred and one pupils. Another was Maidstone Girls' Grammar School, established in 1886 with a grant of £10,000 from the Rochester Bridge Wardens, who through the centuries had accumulated so much money that they asked the Charity Commissioners what they could do with it. The answer was that they should set up a girls' school for Maidstone and Rochester. This was done, and then, as a result of the 1902 act, it became aided from public funds.

Some of the new aided schools were ancient charitable foundations, as for example the Lilley and Stone Foundation, Newark. This had come into existence as the result of two bequests in 1623 and 1688 for poor children of Newark, working in the Jersey School. The girls were taught to spin, the yarn was knitted into stockings by poor widows of Newark, and the Trustees ran the school partly as a business, partly as an educational enterprise. In 1907 land was given by the Duke of Newcastle, and in 1910 the new school, the Newark Girls' High School, was built for £5,000.

Other schools had started as private ventures, such as Stroud Girls' High School. Stroud had long possessed a school for boys, but in 1904 a group of people set up a school for girls, badly housed in the Art School, with one unqualified teacher. In 1909 it was threatened with closure by the Board of Education, but pressure from local people and former pupils persuaded the

County Council to come to the rescue and build a school, which in 1911 absorbed the private school.

These examples show some of the complexities that have persisted at every level in the national system of education. The passing of an Act of Parliament was no magic wand, immediately producing hundreds of identical schools—happily for education, far from it. The Association had to decide on its relationship with the head mistresses of this new range of schools, and it is not surprising that it was a little apprehensive of what it might be admitting to its carefully selected membership. This uncertainty was intensified by the mistrust of the Board of Education and of the local authorities which prevailed at that time. Head mistresses did not see how secondary education could be guided by Education Committees whose members often had "no more than an elementary education." They were puzzled about the admission of scholarship-holders to the schools. What was to be the proportion of these? How were they to be selected? And how absorbed? Some members thought the administration of these different grades of secondary school by local authorities presented insuperable difficulties and foresaw the loss of academic standards.

But these were, on the whole, minority voices, even though some heads of the older schools found it difficult to understand the problems of the new, a difficulty which was to recur after the Act of 1944. In 1906 the heads of the new schools were formally accepted into the membership of the Association. What might have been a deep division was in fact a fresh assertion of unity and equality among the heads of differently governed schools. A few years later Sara Burstall was able to say to the Conference, "The sympathy and tact which is our inheritance as women ought to enable us to bring together the two parties, the old and the new, in Education. . . . We are all drawn together in this one Association to maintain that, however different our schools and our sphere may be, our work is the same." An outstanding instance of the generosity advocated by Sara Burstall was shown by the Guildford High School (founded by the Church Schools Company) which realized after the 1902 Act that it could no longer meet the local need for secondary education for girls. It thereupon gave full consent and co-operation to the opening of the new County

School for Girls, provided the school with its first head mistress, and "by a distribution of duties, all the teaching power required until the new school was fairly on its feet." Many examples could be quoted of head mistresses who gave great encouragement to Education Committees in the formation of rate-aided secondary schools, assisting with their practical knowledge and experience. The fees in the new schools were about half those of the independent high schools, and of course there were free places as well, but although this must have caused the heads some anxiety, it did not deter them from sympathetic action.

Certainly the new County Schools in the first years of their development owed much to their head mistresses, and it was through them that the ethos of the girls' schools continued to develop and spread so that the same ideals inspired schools of many different kinds up and down the country. Many of the heads were young, and represented the new type of qualified teacher who had joined the schools through the 1890s. They came mainly from the universities, and teaching was still the career most readily open to them. They had probably served on the staff of one of the pioneer schools; so that before long there was a network of heads who had shared the daily life of a staff common room and looked forward to meeting again at Conferences and comparing their further experiences. A number of schools became recognized as "nurseries for head mistresses" and could talk proudly of the "daughters of the house." The new secondary schools offered these women an opportunity just when they were ready for it, and they seized it eagerly, almost with a sense of mission. Some chose the strenuous day-schools of the North, whose names were soon to become famous; some preferred to be in or near London, but this was not their Mecca. A small country high school might well have a head mistress as distinguished in her own right as one in the metropolis, and there was no dearth of candidates for any post. Schools which in the 1880s had received about thirty applications of indifferent quality for a headship found that with their new status they could choose from more than a hundred suitable applicants. They could also improve on the salary. One school in 1886 offered a "basic salary of £45 per annum plus a capitation fee of not less than £2 nor more than £4 per pupil at the discretion of the Governors." In 1905 a typical salary was £300, with a capitation fee of £1 for every pupil in excess of one hundred.

Some of the heads, partly owing to youth and inexperience, were at first uncertain about their relationship with the local education authority. They found the air of officialdom foreign, and, tending either to resist or to ignore it, were surprised to discover that they were involved in a clash with bureaucracy. One young head, after an epidemic of colds and coughs in her school, closed it for a couple of days without official leave, although after exchanging a blithe word with her chairman of governors. A startled director tactfully let the enormity pass, but might not have done so. Another head, on being informed that the keeping of a time book by herself and staff had been decreed, first protested unsuccessfully that such a thing was undignified and irrelevant, and thereafter "kept" the book entirely blank until the hated objects were abolished. Yet another, if legend is to be believed, when warned of a visit of inspectors, sent the whole school out to the swimming baths and told the inspector at the front door that no one was at home.

Such incidents illustrate the many-sided adjustments that had to be made if the new era was to be a success. To learn how to find a balance between much-prized freedom and acceptance of authority was not an easy lesson. It was learnt only through patience and goodwill on all sides, and the ability of both officials and head mistresses to see beyond the "present discontents" to the goal which was their common objective. Fortunately there were at hand head mistresses of character and vision who were able to take their share in this undertaking. One example was Margaret Powell (Orme Girls' School), the daughter of a parson who was a classical scholar, educated at home and the eldest of a large family. When her mother died she stayed at home to look after the others, but at the age of forty went to Newnham and obtained a First Class in the Classical Tripos. She taught for only four years, and then went to Orme, retiring in 1919 at the age of seventy-two. Until her day the girls had all been addressed as "Miss" so-and-so, but she introduced Christian names and enlightened practices such as taking the sixth form in small groups of two or three to Wales or the Lake District, to walk, talk and sketch. It soon became evident that she was offering service far beyond the terms of her appointment, and that her chief concern was to widen the opportunities presented to the girls and to educate them as citizens.

Another was K. Scotson Clark who in 1901 became head mistress of the tiny private school at Allerton, continued when it became an independent school, and remained as head when it was taken over by the Leeds City Council in 1914. She retired in 1931, the head of a school of 351 pupils, with a great reputation. She must have had a striking presence, for two descriptions reveal the impression she made on the pupils. One of them recalls, "At five I went to a new school. Miss Scotson Clark, the head mistress, was seven or eight feet high, dressed from neck to toe in black, ornamented with a frontal fin of agate buttons like very black shiny currants. She was as graceful as a dolphin." The second personal recollection recaptures the atmosphere of the time, "In January 1926 a dance was held to celebrate the school's twenty-fifth birthday. Past and present pupils and interested friends were told on the invitation card, 'Fancy or Evening Dress, Games and Conjuror. March Past. Dancing. Boys and girls up to the age of seventeen are invited to stay till 9 o'clock, after which there will be dancing for those above that age. Carriages at 11.30.' Miss Clark looked superb in a beautiful crinoline dress. In school she always wore black with a boned-lace neckline, but at the Ball she had a very low neck and a superb carriage. She took my childish breath away"! Another outstanding character was Frances Mary Nodes, an assistant at Brondesbury and Kilburn High School and then a Training College lecturer, who spent twenty years as head mistress of Doncaster High School. At her second Speech Day in 1906 she said, "We do not exist for the purpose of getting girls through any particular examination, nor do we draw up our curriculum with examinations in view. On the contrary, we discourage, as far as possible, work done solely with a view to coming examinations, and try as far as we can to give the girls a wide and liberal culture which will fit them for life, rather than for any particular calling."

Many women appointed as the first head mistresses of the county secondary schools, remained for a long spell of years in the same post, and with all the new ground to be broken this continuity was a great boon to the schools. It is interesting to note the dates of some of their terms of service: 1874-1910, 1891-1914, 1906-30, 1901-31, 1907-27. During that time, many of the schools grew from about fifty or eighty pupils to four or five hundred. Many of them outgrew their first makeshift habitations and moved into new purpose-built buildings. With the 1914-18 war they passed out of one era into another, and in many instances the same head mistress was with them as they moved.

One of the most eminent of these head mistresses was Grace Fanner, a distinguished scholar of Newnham College, who gained a First Class in the Cambridge Moral Sciences Tripos in 1894 and a First in the Modern Languages Tripos in 1895. As Cambridge did not at that time grant degrees she took her MA at Dublin University. For eight years she was on the staff of the independent Church of England High School, Eaton Square. From 1903 to 1907 she was Head of Sale High School, and in 1907 was appointed the first head mistress of Putney County Secondary School, where she remained until 1934. She soon made her mark in the Association and was the first head of a maintained school to become President. Another outstanding figure was Alice M. Stoneman, the first head mistress of the Park School, Preston, where she reigned from 1907 to 1930. She was educated at the North London Collegiate School (where her mother had been one of the first pupils), from which she won a mathematical scholarship to Girton College, Cambridge, but changed over to Classics for her Tripos. She also took the MA degree of Trinity College, Dublin, and was an assistant mistress at Rochester High School when she was appointed to the Park School. Her successor, Kathleen Reynolds, writes, "she was a dominant and dynamic character, and though she firmly believed, in theory, in considerable freedom in school, in practice it did not always work out that way, if she thought the standard might slip. Her intellect was powerful, for she thought twice as quickly as others, and saw three moves ahead of anybody else. When she entered a room she radiated power, usually dominating the occasion, with quick and witty, sometimes caustic, retorts and brilliant repartee. . . ." Obviously not an easy or comfortable personality but she "fought relentlessly" for the cause of girls' education and had the distinction of being made a Life Member of the Association. The early head mistresses had been devotees of the bicycle. Their successors in the 1930s, when they were no longer young, gaily took to the wheel of the motor-car, and Alice Stoneman was an intrepid and alarming driver. Her love of speed, and determination never to be thwarted, terrified those whom she took out with her "as a treat." She never learnt to reverse and her remark, "I like to go forward, not backwards," might be taken as symbolic of her life and character.

It is symbolic, too, of many of her contemporaries, for although Grace Fanner and Alice Stoneman were unusually strong personalities, they are typical of a number of head mistresses of that era, who helped to create the maintained girls' schools. They made a tremendous impact on the neighbourhood, bringing with them the traditions and educational standards which by then were accepted in the schools where they had been teaching. Often they were answerable to a board of governors, who, though exceedingly proud of their new school and anxious for its success, knew little of the world of education and were quite ignorant of how to carry out their task. The local officials also were new to their job, prone to make mistakes, and one of the first duties of the head was to take her share in building up confidence and trust and to win the respect and understanding of the neighbourhood for this new type of girls' education. She was sometimes the key figure, the personal link between the different official bodies. Here continuity was of special value because all were engaged on a common enterprise, working it out from the start, and gradually they got to know each other and a partnership was established. Parents and governors discovered that the head mistress was no narrow-minded blue-stocking, but a woman of wide interests and deep humanity, formidable certainly at times, but able to speak with knowledge and insight, one on whose judgement and sympathy they could rely.

There are many former pupils of these schools, who have held responsible posts up and down the country, and managed their own homes, who if asked what they remember best about their head mistress give the same answer, "She cared about every one of us; she knew all about us, and was determined that everyone should have her chance. I owe everything that I have done to her." If the girl was promising academically the head mistress interviewed her father or mother and insisted that she should go to a university or training college, rescuing her almost as a brand from the burning. A crying need in most instances was for money, and her efforts to secure this was one thing which brought the head into touch with people of influence in the neighbourhood, men and women, some of whom were still suspicious of this new education for girls. When they discovered how deeply the head mistress was concerned with the welfare of the local girls, they were ready to help, either personally or with grants from business firms, or by creating an endowment fund. This was one of the ways by which understanding and confidence were gradually established, resulting often in a lifelong friendship between benefactor and head mistress.

Of course there were black spots, for universal sweetness and light were hardly to be expected. Some authorities were rigidly bureaucratic and illiberal: some head mistresses could not be protected from their own follies, but the story of the schools established as a result of the 1902 Act is a remarkable one. The women who became head mistresses of those schools were not only engaged in carrying the education of girls a stage further, but were taking part in a national venture. The schools which were most successful were those where there was a real partnership between the local authority, the governing body, the inspectorate and the head mistress. It was this partnership which produced a new understanding of what secondary education could achieve.

Chapter 5

Assertions

The years between 1902 and the First World War saw a gradual expansion, both in the nature and activity of the Association itself and in the educational thought and experiment going on amongst its members.

Numerically the Association was growing. From 1901 to 1906 its numbers rose from 180 to 230, and with the admission, in 1906, of the heads of the "new" secondary schools this growth was accelerated. It had doubled by 1912. Geographically also there was expansion. Every part of the country had its members, as well as every type of school. Wales indeed had been in the vanguard in this respect, having had, since the Welsh Intermediate Act of 1889, its own system of secondary grammar schools. Even in the last ten years of the nineteenth century there were eight Welsh secondary schools in membership, and in May 1902 Osmond Williams, member for Merionethshire, speaking in the Commons, quoted the words of a Welshman who "wondered how it was you English did not envy the stream of higher educational influence flowing like running brooks by every cottage and farm through all the hills and valleys of Scotland and Wales, and try to emulate it." "On the contrary," added Mr Williams, "you do not appear to think at all of secondary education as a living influence and a power which ought to form a beneficent part of the actual life of the people." In 1935 in Wales 223 children out of every thousand were receiving secondary education, as compared with 119 in England, and this proportion was reflected in the Association's membership. In Scotland, with the deeply-rooted tradition of co-education (and consequently of headmastership), things were different. Not until the early years of this century were head mistresses appointed to such schools as those of the Merchant Company in Edinburgh. Scottish membership has thus been numerically small, though important, and during the period in question it was increasing.

Two other developments in the Association during this period are worth noting, for both show the same intent to widen scope and opportunity which was the essence of those years. One—although its full realization belongs rather to the years after the war of 1914—was the acceptance into membership of the head mistresses of schools run by the religious orders, mostly Roman Catholic. Their numbers have grown steadily and are now in the region of one hundred and thirty. They take an increasingly active part in discussion and decision at all levels.

The other was the decision, no less significant, taken in 1909, to offer either full or "correspondent" membership to heads of girls' schools in British Colonies and Dependencies overseas. By 1915 there were fourteen members in these two categories—a number which was to rise year by year to over sixty by 1970—with a geographical spread which looks almost global, including head mistresses in Australia, Canada, New Zealand, the Argentine, many parts of Africa, Malaysia, Hong Kong. This extension in space has, like other extensions, been a double advantage to the Association. In its early stages it was difficult for a head mistress ten thousand miles away to share her experience and her problems with her professional colleagues in the United Kingdom. Now, when travel is speedy and universal, members are sure of a ready welcome in all parts of the world. They can also look forward to meeting each other at the annual Conference. In addition to schools in full membership, there are six Overseas Affiliated Associations, an illustration of the out-going character of the Association, which became a marked feature as its international interests developed.

All these extensions of membership had a profound and invigorating effect. From being a small and homogeneous body the Association came to include a wide variety among its members—a variety of background, of convictions, of local setting. The lively intercommunication of ideas which this produced was a factor in the quality of this period's thinking.

Ideas were communicated also by participation in the administrative side of education outside the school. By 1904 forty members had been invited to serve on Education Committees, a fulfilment of Jane Connolly's presidential advice in 1903 to "take your full share in the public educational work of the day." In 1903 a special Conference on Educational Questions, convened by the Association of Head Mistresses was held in Haberdashers' Hall, to be followed by one in the Clothworkers' Hall in 1905, and another in 1909. These were important occasions, bringing together chairmen and members of Education Committees, representatives of universities and of women's colleges, head mistresses, and others "directly or indirectly concerned with the establishment and government of girls' schools, and who may have a share in the settlement of educational questions of first-rate importance." The Conferences were formally received by the Master of the Company in whose hall they were meeting, the President of the Association took the chair, and the frank discussions were of a high order. The agenda gave opportunity for valuable exchange of thought on such topics as: The Administrative side of Education, The Awarding of Scholarships, Training of Teachers, Technical Education and Open-air Industries, Co-education, Principles of Curricula, The Establishment of Different Types of Schools by Local Education Authorities, and other matters impinging on many different aspects of education. Robert Morant attended the 1905 Conference although his relationships with head mistresses were distinctly strained at the time. Michael Sadler was the invited speaker. The conferences must have fostered understanding and co-operation over some of the burning questions of the day, and their records are a tribute to the initiative and imagination of the Association.

In 1904 the fears of the head mistresses over the possible tyranny of the 1902 Act had been revived when they were faced with the new Regulations for Secondary Schools, signed in that year by Robert Morant. These laid down the exact subjects to be included in the school course and the minimum number of hours to be spent on the different groups at each stage, ". . . not less than 7½ hours to Science and Mathematics, of which at least 3 must be for Science. . . . When two languages other than English are taken and Latin is not one of them, the Board will require to be satisfied that the omission of Latin is for the advantage of the School . . . ," etc. These strict directions were partly due to Morant's desire to differentiate clearly between the elementary and secondary schools: he was dubious about the work being done in the higher grade elementary schools (some of which were now to become secondary) and wanted to safeguard the grammar school curriculum.

To the head mistresses, however, such instructions seemed an outrage. Not only were they unaccustomed to having these matters dictated from above, but they held their own strong views on the curriculum and had expounded them in public on many occasions. They did not coincide with those of Robert Morant. In addition to this, these strictures and the enforced allocation of teaching time made impossible the use of "free afternoons" for recreation, the arts, or private study, all of which the head mistresses considered necessary for the development of the "whole child." They joined readily in the battle which followed the publication of the regulations, acting however with exemplary propriety. At the July Executive of 1904 the Educational Administration Committee of the Association was asked to prepare a memorandum which was then considered by the full Executive and presented to the Board in the following December; it was followed up by a personal deputation in February 1905. The memorandum contained this paragraph, "The head mistresses feel . . . that the amount of freedom hitherto allowed them was a vital condition of the introduction and fostering of the many improvements in organization and methods which they have successfully carried out in their schools and they would, therefore, deplore the issue of rigid rules and regulations which would hamper their initiative, lessen their sense of responsibility, and force uniformity upon them. If the schools become stereotyped and can no longer be brought into line with the special needs of the neighbourhood in which they are placed, the education given in them, and their prestige, must in numerous cases be affected, and not for good."

In 1907 the detailed prescription of the timetable was

renounced and in bringing this about the head mistresses had played their part, and had declared their right to think for themselves in matters of education.

And to think for themselves was exactly what they were doing. The new county schools were, to a striking degree, proving their quality and justifying their place in the system of education, and the variety they brought to membership of the Association was in itself a stimulus to fresh thinking, and to the exchange of new ideas and experiences.

The head mistresses took nothing for granted. They were intelligent women, realists, with lively minds, and they turned their attention to one topic after another, often seeing with disconcerting clarity the flaws in existing educational practices or in new proposals.

They published a pamphlet on "The True Cost of Secondary Education for Girls," analysing the claims of salaries, buildings, upkeep and working expenses, and comparing English practices with those of other countries. In connection with this they went on to join with the Association of Assistant Mistresses in drawing up acceptable conditions for the engagement or employment of staff in girls' secondary schools. This is only one example of the close co-operation which has always existed between these two bodies, and the valuable results which joint action has produced.

They gave the Board of Education no rest over the "limitations of sphere and inferiority of status" assigned to women in the Inspectorate, taking the initiative in arranging for an influential deputation to be received by the President of the Board in March 1909, on the "Position of Women Inspectors under the Board of Education." They refused to appoint a representative on a Committee of King's College, London, to organize special courses for the higher education of women in Home Science and Economics, because "the formation of classes with a man as director and lecturer seemed to the Executive Committee of the Association of Head Mistresses an initial error."

They sent two delegates to the Third International Congress on School Hygiene which met in Paris in 1910. On their return they reported that, "two points were specially insisted on: (1) Overwork is a serious danger and *must* be stopped. (2) Sexual instruction must be given in schools." The delegates heartily agreed with the first motion, but although agreeing in principle with the second, "because parents so often failed" to give the instruction, were "not convinced that such instruction should be given in classes." In the same year the Association formed a committee "for the supervision of University Girl Students," to look into conditions of residence, systems of registration, provision made for illness, and other such matters.

They had representatives serving on the Federal Council of Secondary School Associations, supporting the efforts to form a Teachers' Registration Council and set up a register. Several times those engaged in the struggle seemed to be on the brink of success—as for instance at the Conference in 1909, under the chairmanship of Herbert Hardy Cozens-Hardy, Master of the Rolls, but even·this superlative effort ended in failure, and the Teachers' Register has not come into existence yet.

The Association had always refused to get embroiled in party politics, and although individuals such as Dorinda Neligan had been active suffragettes, the official policy of the Association was "No action." During these years, however, it felt compelled to express its views in order to reveal the political situation of educated women. In 1906 and 1909 it declared its approval of women's suffrage in principle. In 1909 a petition signed by 223 members was sent to H.H. Asquith, the Prime Minister. It complained that "Unlike the head master the head mistress is relegated to the same class as the male convict and lunatic; she may—nay must—do the work of a citizen, but may not have a citizen's privileges." It went on, "We desire enfranchisement for the protection of our sex, of girls' schools, of our profession, but above all . . . we desire to see the whole work of the country perfected, as it can only be when the gifts of women as well as those of men can be freely given for its service."

An important matter which caused much heart-searching was the question of free places in aided secondary schools, to be awarded by the local authorities to children attending element-ary schools. Sophie Bryant, addressing the Conference on Educational Questions in 1904, supported the idea, speaking with her usual sympathy and insight, but the reaction to her speech showed that some members were by no means recon-ciled to admitting these scholars. Edith Creak feared the danger of having the schools "flooded" with such children, unable to pass the ordinary examinations, and felt that "the taking of elementary school children from the Board school to the University is often a most mischievous action. There could hardly be a greater cruelty to the children. 'Lift them by all means; do not think I have any class prejudices, but the strain is cruel.' " Stating that there were 150 elementary school scholars in the Birmingham grammar schools, she added, "I have no hesitation in saying that the money might just as well be thrown into the sea." The general discussion, however, showed a better understanding of the problem, and dealt not only with minor but also intermediate and major scholarships: it was clear that the majority of administrators and head mistresses were working together to overcome the inevitable failures in the initial stages of the scheme.

Another subject which claimed its full share of attention was co-education, especially in the years 1904 and 1905 when it formed a major item of discussion at Executive Committees and Conferences. Many Education Committees, in order to carry out their obligations under the Act, were contemplating the establishment of co-educational or mixed schools, and at the Educational Conference in 1905 the Chairman of the Southend Higher Education Sub-committee stated, "With regard to the special circumstances of co-education, the financial question stands first in a district such as ours. In a town such as Southend it would be impracticable to establish separate schools. If the Secondary School were limited to either boys or girls, one of the sexes would have to do without a school. Therefore co-education was the only practical alternative." This hard fact lay behind the establishment of most of these schools, but many points for consideration were put forward by the Executive of the Association of Head Mistresses and discussed at length. The following arguments were amongst those covered. The status of the woman teacher would suffer; the heads of such schools were sure to be men, obviously not in the best interests of girls and unjust to women, who, whatever their academic position would be relegated to subordinate posts; the curriculum would be under the control of a head master, and therefore presumably more suited to boys—leading perhaps to overstrain on girls in their efforts to keep abreast. Great stress was laid on the need for the care and authority of a woman over girls in their adolescent years, and fears were expressed that in a mixed school the interests of the girls in curriculum, character and health would take second place.

Sophie Bryant remarked, "It is not enough, when a man is the head of a school to place a woman under him as chief assistant, and to say that she is responsible for the girls; for she cannot be responsible unless she can be independent of him." The experience of co-education in the United States was frequently referred to, either as a dreadful warning or as a desirable ideal. In spite of the protests of the Association of Head Mistresses, mixed schools continued to increase, and the Association continued to do battle. They passed resolutions expressing their views and they issued a memorandum entitled *Mixed Secondary Schools under the Headship of a Man,* containing six definite recommendations. In 1913 a joint deputation of head mistresses, assistant mistresses, and the Education Committee of the National Union of Women Workers waited on the Board of Education and stated their opinions. All through the controversy the head mistresses made it clear that they were speaking of mixed schools, under the headship of a man, established for motives of economy, and not about co-educational schools founded to carry out certain definite educational theories. To-day, when the issue has once more forced itself on the attention of head mistresses, it is interesting to compare the arguments.

It was, however, matters relating to the curriculum which most appealed to the head mistresses and absorbed their interest. They held strong views on the length of school hours, the claims of home which must not be ignored, the necessity of leaving time for the development of special gifts and for independent study.

By the turn of the century the standard of girls seeking admission to the secondary schools had greatly improved, and the heads no longer had to struggle, as in the early days, with those who were without even the first rudiments of education. They chose, however, to admit girls of varying ability, always with the proviso that they could benefit from the type of education offered, and after the Act of 1902 the range was extended. The heads were very conscious of their duty towards girls of every type, and they had specialist committees working on all the subjects in the curriculum, and drawing up suggested syllabuses. Eliza Woodhouse (Clapham High School) made this the main theme of her presidential address to the annual Conference in 1909. She spoke of the possibility of a "Reformed Timetable," particularly for the girls from sixteen to eighteen, when there was need to differentiate between the "College girl" who would proceed to a university or to a professional career, and the "Non-College Girl" who had no such aspirations, but who must be prevented from becoming merely a poor copy of the more scholastic type. To quote some of her words, "At no time can there be any pause in educational reform, and . . . in this matter of curriculum, voluntary reform on our part is preferable to forced change brought about through external compulsion. . . . this is the age when we should offer a wide range of alternative courses to meet individual tastes and varying circumstances."

In connection with this reform, Domestic Science was subject to fresh scrutiny and given a "new look." In 1908 King's College, London, began to provide various courses in Home Science and Economics, to fit women for responsible posts in industry, and to qualify them for teaching, a sign of the movement that was taking place in favour of improved training for girls in the home arts. It was clear that a grounding in Science was more important than knowing how to make a Charlotte russe and that a scientific basis was what the schools ought to be providing. "There must be an adjustment of relationship between science proper and domestic science." This in turn led to an investigation of the syllabuses in Physics and Chemistry required in external examination and these were soon the subject of attack. They were "too abstract," planned for boys' and men's industries, with no direct relation to the girl's later work in life—they must be altered. Applied science was what was needed, and a resolution was passed to that effect. As Edith Leahy (Croydon High School) said, "Let the boys take it too."

Art and Music had not been neglected in the girls' schools, but now they were given a more prominent place, and at least one of the Arts was to be studied with "quickening interest" in the suggested two-year course. The amount of ground covered by the Association during these years was extraordinary, and one is constantly struck by the bold and realistic approach of the head mistresses. "Relation to life" was a recurring phrase. They fought for freedom in making their own timetables, and against compulsion of any kind. They considered that "specialization in girls' education was a great national question, and head mistresses should be the first to ask for needed reforms."

The subject of religious education claimed a great deal of thought and reassessment, no longer to be viewed mainly from the angle of religious conscience but as an important and integral part in a whole education. "Scripture" could not, to many minds, still be the simple Biblical instruction of an earlier day. The climate of general thought and criticism (and these were the days of the so-called Higher Criticism) was changing in the direction of a more scholarly and impersonal approach. Although in nearly all schools, whether based on a "religious" foundation or not, there was a concern for religion, opinion varied widely on how this could be "taught" as a subject. Should it be the responsibility of the form mistress? Or of a specialist teacher? Should it be a subject for examination? At the Conference of 1904 these questions were raised and fully discussed. Two years later, the Executive Committee resolved "to approach universities and other bodies with reference to the establishment of special certificates to qualify teachers to give instruction in schools in Religious Knowledge"; but much time was to pass before the idea of specialist teaching was fully accepted. One head mistress recalls a rapid exchange at a discussion of this subject at a Branch meeting many years later. Miss X., with calm certainty, "Scholarship is the chief requirement"; Miss Y., with passion, "The letter killeth, the spirit giveth life"; Miss X., swiftly, "The devil can cite Scripture for his purpose."

A characteristic of girls' schools had been, from the start, the concern shown by head mistresses for the care of health and all that it implied. At first there had been real anxiety in case unaccustomed study should result in undue strain, and parents and critics had grave misgivings, particularly with regard to public examinations and their effect on the nervous system. The topic was constantly discussed at meetings, the need for exercise fully recognized, and many experiments introduced. In

1898 Frances Dove (Wycombe Abbey School) enthusiastically advocated, "Let us have games of all kinds, lawn tennis, fives, bowls, croquet, quoits, golf, swimming, skating, archery, tobogganing, basket-ball, rounders and hailes; some at one season of the year, others at another."

All amateur ideas, however, were swept away with the advent of the Physical Training Colleges and the reign of the physical training mistress. The Madame Osterberg College at Dartford was founded in 1885, the Ling Association in 1899, Bedford Physical Training College in 1903; and as the trained specialists filtered into the schools a transformation took place. Drill and callisthenics gave way to physical training, to become in its turn the all-embracing physical education. Head mistresses, ahead of their day in the importance they had attached to the matter,

Not everyone was
enthusiastic about
the cult of PE
(By permission of
The Times Educational
Supplement)

gave every support to the colleges, and welcomed their students. The physical training mistress became a power in the land. She brought to the schools a basic knowledge of health and hygiene, a trained mind and a high concept of her responsibilities. Medical inspection became a recognized feature of the girls' schools, to be followed up by preventive and remedial treatment; the girls acquired a self-reliance which was apparent in their deportment, the way they moved about the school, and in their greatly improved alertness and response.

Organized games were not in the original tradition but in 1909 Frances Gray (St Paul's Girls' School) opened a discussion at the annual Conference on "The Right and Wrong of Games," declaring in her first sentence that she would rule out of consideration the right and confine herself to the wrong. In 1911, in a book entitled *Public Schools for Girls*, which set out schemes for most of the subjects in the curriculum, a head mistress stated that organized games were by then "provided in all girls' schools which have any pretensions to efficiency." In boarding schools they were usually compulsory; in day schools the practice varied. St Leonard's School, at St Andrews, and Roedean are mentioned as being two of the first schools to become notable for their prowess in games. The whole system was adopted with conscientious thoroughness, and in some schools it became almost a tyranny. Even the head mistress might quail when confronted with the expert assurance of the teacher of physical training, and give way to her demands. Girls jumped to obey her slightest orders, and revelled in the whole paraphernalia of team colours, form and house matches, and other competitive events. Exactness over uniform was sometimes carried to extremes, and great importance attached to the precise length of a tunic, and such details as the width of hair-ribbons and the exact placing of a tie-pin on the middle stripe of a tie. This was the great day of team photographs, and cheerful girls, sometimes adorned with the oddest headgear, grasped their rackets or sticks and boldly faced the world.

The Swedish System which was then followed in the majority of schools tended towards regimentation, marching in step, and massed displays, but this phase was to change and pass on through rhythmic movement and group work to the great variety of activities now found in the schools. These include dance, athletics, free movement of all kinds, and games which call particularly for individual skill and are socially acceptable out of school; they are much more in keeping with modern tastes.

During the first few decades of the twentieth century the girls' grammar schools were in a state of remarkable development and their standards were high. The excellence of a school was an individual matter and schools of outstanding merit as well as some of indifferent quality were to be found in every sector, whether maintained or independent. The head mistresses believed that "learning should be a part of living, and even the necessity of fitting boys and girls to earn a livelihood must be subordinated to the idea of a good life." The schools were not to be forcing-houses for the intellectual girl, but pleasant places, retaining a sense of leisure and freedom and enjoyment in the work being done. Such a philosophy was practicable because neither the head nor the school was subject to the same relentless pressures as now assail them. Life moved at a slower tempo, and there was time to think, in spite of the words of Mary Douglas (Godolphin School, Salisbury). Even in that quiet cathedral city she felt, "We all feel the rush of these racing, all too full days . . . even we who live in the country find everything going so fast that it is difficult to do anything well. . . ." Little did she know how the pace was to quicken in the next fifty years.

The boarding schools had changed greatly since their early struggling days and were enjoying a period of unrivalled prosperity, meeting in particular the needs of parents whose work lay overseas. In 1919 the Association formed a sub-committee, "to consider matters concerning boarding schools and school boarding houses," and in 1921 "The Association for Head Mistresses of Boarding Schools" came into being. Many of the boarding schools were organized in separate houses, on the lines of boys' public schools, and were comfortable though not luxurious establishments. Domestic labour was abundant, matrons and resident staff of good quality easy to find. The house mistress reigned supreme in her own domain, treated as "the lady of the house" and great attention was given to training the girls in manners and morals. Most girls (with, of course, exceptions) enjoyed the communal life, and happily absorbed the traditions and public spirit.

"And try to project an image more in keeping with your status symbol."

(By permission of Punch)

In every sector of the secondary school field, girls' education flourished, stimulated by the fact that the schools were engaged primarily on the business of education, not yet harassed by major changes in organization. A head mistress had no need to justify her work as in the early days, or to be unduly sensitive to public criticism (publicity was a menace which was to return later in a different guise). She had her accepted place in the community in which she lived, and farther afield if she wished to seek it. In her school she was probably still a little aloof, but in the main her staff were colleagues rather than subordinates, although in the staff-room a strict hierarchy might prevail. Any suggestion of uniformity in dress had long since disappeared and the head expressed her personal taste in this as in other matters. Some found satisfaction in extending their home life, helping with the education of young nieces and nephews who lived with them in term-time, or adopting children for whom they took entire responsibility. Some wrote books or articles and cultivated their intellectual and artistic talents. Foreign travel was a favourite form of refreshment and they enjoyed holidays abroad, studying the language and browsing happily in galleries and museums: from these expeditions they brought back reproductions of pictures and works of art which graced the rooms and corridors of their schools, reminders of a wider culture. This was in keeping with their belief that no school, whether girls' or boys', should be a bare and depressing place, but that it should be made attractive by "beauty of pictures, flowers, seemliness and grace of domestic detail."

A head mistress was still in most cases required to do a good deal of teaching, but this was no hardship as it was probably as a teacher that she had made her mark, and often a school would excel in the head mistress's specialist subject and become widely known on that account. When it came to organization, she often worked in the light of nature. In a task so absorbing as the work of a head mistress, skill and experience are needed in order to achieve "a margin of attention as well as time," and not every head had the wisdom to follow Mary Clarke's later advice on the head's duty to give freedom to her staff by delegation, "Do nothing yourself that you can get someone else to do for you." A head would almost certainly consider it her duty to make the timetable, even though this might have disastrous results. One, continually hard-pressed, is said to have acquired disconcerting habits in interviews with prospective staff, usually walking them round and round Trafalgar Square. Another, prone to absent-mindedness, was apt to forget the interviews she had arranged, and a former member of her staff has a vivid recollection of her own experience. She found herself accompanying the head mistress to a meeting she was due to attend on the other side of the town, desperately shouting out her personal credentials above the clanging of the tram-car, where they sat swaying side by side.

During these years revolution was more in evidence than reluctance, and in the developments taking place the Association was fortunate in its leaders. Several of these have already been mentioned. There were others, still young, who were later to hold the office of President, whose opinions were beginning to count in the counsels of the Association. Amongst them were Edith Major (King Edward's High School, Birmingham), later Mistress of Girton College, Frances Gray, Beatrice Sparks (Colston's Girls' School, Bristol) and Lucy Lowe (Leeds Girls' High School).

One of the most eminent of those already holding office was Sophie Bryant (North London Collegiate School) who was President from 1903 to 1905 and after her retirement remained a vice-president until 1922. She was a keen mountaineer and it was at Chamonix in that year that she died while climbing. Her distinguished academic career has already been mentioned, and although she obtained most of her qualifications while working as a full-time teacher, she won honours and prizes at every stage. She was the first head mistress to take her place on national committees and commissions, being a member of the Royal Commission on Secondary Education under the chairmanship of James Bryce in 1894; she was the first woman to be elected by Convocation to the Senate of the University of London a member of the Consultative Committee of the Board of Education in 1900, of the Education Committee of the London County Council from 1904 to 1910, and in 1908 Chairman of the Executive Committee formed to deal with the great meeting in London of the first International Congress for Moral Instruction in Schools.

Wherever she served she made her mark, and her exceptional ability was soon recognized. Michael Sadler, speaking of her work on the Bryce Commission, wrote, "Many a formidable cloud upon our Chairman's brow have I seen melt under the sunshine of Mrs Bryant's face and her beguiling words. . . . none of us could manage him as she did. . . . one could not fail to admire the practical good sense of her brave idealism. . . . Mrs Bryant allowed us all to feel that we had become her friends, and our friendship deepened with the experience and fellow-service of later years."

This combination of "practical good sense and brave idealism" was apparent in many of her speeches to the Association, which owed much to her guidance in its own internal affairs as well as to the way in which she enhanced its reputation with the general public. Other head mistresses, in later years, were to have the same kind of influence and position, but she was one of the first.

It is easy to use the term "modern" and it has many shades of meaning, but the ideas put forward by the head mistresses of that era were sufficiently modern to be relevant to educational thought to-day. To quote a few sentences from Sophie Bryant's statement, made in 1904, of her educational philosophy: "Once the interest of the child is aroused, the studies and duties corresponding begin to run of themselves. The beginning of sound education, therefore, consists in the development of children's interest in all sorts of humanly interesting things. A mind that grows up with such a sphere of interest in it has ready possibilities of contact with other minds, is therefore deeply human, even when comparatively ignorant, and thus predisposed to sympathy with social ends. We easily fail to realize the world-wide horizon of the child's natural desire for knowledge. . . . In our concern about set lessons and definite acquisition, we are only too apt to forget the glorious, though somewhat incapable, versatility of the child, and thus to neglect the development of that interest in all the vast miscellaneous world, which is the prime universal requisite of intellectual education. . . ." This was in 1904. In 1974 the statement is equally acceptable.

Chapter 6

The two world wars

Into this period of expansion and development came the First World War of 1914-18. R.A. Butler in *The Art of the Possible* wrote, "It is remarkable how, in England, educational planning and advance have coincided with war," and as an example he instanced the Fisher Act of 1918, many of whose reforming proposals unhappily were later "killed by the economic blizzard which was to freeze the educational pattern for most of the inter-war years." The 1914-18 war, in spite of its enormous general impact, did not seriously arrest the developments in education already under way. It is true that many children suffered acutely from family losses of fathers and brothers or from shortages of food and clothing, but because no areas were turned into deserts of rubble by bombing, and few schools were destroyed or commandeered, they did not lose much formal education, as thousands of children did in the Second World War. The war certainly deepened the sense of responsibility—both within the teaching profession and outside it—for the present education and the future well-being of the young. It also had the further effect of sharpening public awareness of world problems and world relations. It was this heightened awareness which led first to the setting up of the junior branches of the League of Nations Union, and later, in 1939, to the founding of the Council for Education in World Citizenship by a group of people which included Gilbert Murray, Lilian Charlesworth (Sutton High School) and B.W. Baker (Badminton School). Lilian Charlesworth succeeded Gilbert Murray as Chairman of the Council in 1953, an office she held with distinction for fourteen years. The Council owed much to her inspiration and drive and her deep concern for people. It was a time when links were greatly strengthened with teacher organizations overseas such as the International Federation of Secondary Teachers (FIPESO), which the Association joined in 1931. And it was a time when many women seeking opportunities of service turned to teaching, not because it was any longer the sole career open to them, but in preference to others. In the years between the wars head mistresses could fill posts with well-qualified teachers of high calibre with none of the desperate searches and contrivances that lay ahead.

The development of girls' education up to the First World War, and after it, differed in pace rather than in nature, and the same was true of the Association. In both periods new ideas and experiments were in the air and the Association did not lack leaders in either. Some of this current liberal thinking was expressed in a book published in 1937 with the somewhat apocalyptic title *The Head Mistress Speaks*. Here Ethel Strudwick (St Paul's Girls' School), urged a unified system of education and defined the aim of the schools, "to create a democracy of tolerance and mutual understanding." Here Christine Arscott (Whalley Range High School, Manchester) deplored "the incalculable waste of highly intelligent children to whom the doors of the secondary school never opened" and she forecast with remarkable accuracy the development of "modern" schools side by side with grammar, with transfer from one to the other. Ethel Ruth Gwatkin (Streatham Hill High School) advocated free secondary education for all, its nature and length depending solely on the needs and aptitudes of the individual. Mary Clarke (Manchester High School), pursuing a line of thought very familiar in the Association, made a plea for freedom in the curriculum. "If modern education for girls," she said, "has created some problems it has solved others. Its growth and spread since the turn of the century has had one most welcome result, a growing freedom of curriculum to suit individual tastes and aptitudes. This could happen the more easily in a movement that was new and unhampered by tradition and it may well prove to be the most distinctive contribution of women to education."

Dorothy Brock (Mary Datchelor School), one of the most humane and persuasive of women, "who took music and Greek to Camberwell" and made her school one of the most musical in England, wrote of the need to combine freedom with tradition and music with the classics. Muriel Davies (Streatham County School), the pioneer of the Dalton plan for independent study, urged the reduction of pressure in education and described her own practice of setting aside some portion of each day for free and un-timetabled work. She believed ardently in partnership and co-operation, and self-government on the lines of a family group "which brings big and little into a natural relationship with each other." Hannah Lister (Selhurst Grammar School, Croydon) expressed faith in the experience of democracy which a school council can give. Looking ahead, she urged the value of what is now familiar as "continuous assessment" and of close contacts with parents, with or without a formal association. Lucy Savill, also true to the traditions of her forerunners, expounded the theme of "differentness" and diversity. She insisted too that every head mistress should evolve a philosophy of education and be prepared to discuss this with the governors, especially when being interviewed, instead of joining in "the usual concerted effort to keep on saying nothing" and getting the job "on the strength of paper qualifications and a good hat."

But besides the thirteen head mistresses who "spoke" in this book there were, of course, many others who gave a lead to their colleagues and in education generally. Among them were Emmeline Tanner (Roedean), her career divided between the maintained and the independent sectors, Dorothy de Zouche (Wolverhampton High School), a scholar and a wit as well as a far-seeing educator, Margaret Adams (Croydon High School) with her tireless enthusiasm for international co-operation and her dauntless refusal to be baulked by obstacles in the way of it, and Agnes Catnach (Putney County School) whose slogan when embarking on any new endeavour was, "It's a challenge," and who was never known to refuse any challenge in the cause of education.

The general trend was towards liberality both educational and social, whether expressed in words or quietly practised, even though individual diehards existed like the head mistress

"Festina lente! Sursum corda! Nil desperandum!"

(By permission of Punch)

who told a member of her staff just appointed to a school in the
East End of London that she was committing social suicide!
There was a growing conviction of the importance of the
individual, of whatever class, station, or ability, of the importance of the child as a whole person, not as a member of
segments to be tenuously connected through the mysteries of
"transference of training." There was in some quarters a strong
resistance to the tyranny of examinations, and the Association,
which had set up its own Examinations Committee in 1907, was
in the forefront of demands for their reform. The School
Certificate, instituted by the Board of Education in 1917 in
place of "a dense jungle of unco-ordinated examinations and
examining bodies," was awarded only to candidates who gained
a minimum of five passes, at least one in a subject taken from

each of three groups—English subjects, Languages, Mathematics and Science. There was a fourth group covering Music, Art, Housecraft and Manual work, but passes in these could not count among the essential five. The main reason for this discrimination was said to be that these subjects were only beginning to gain ground in the schools and an examination might injure their development, but one detects behind this the opinion of the universities, who considered Group Four subjects as highly suspect and quite lacking in discipline. The head mistresses heartily disliked these cramping restrictions, not only because Group Four subjects, though they might indeed only just be becoming respectable in boys' schools, were already well established and flourishing among girls (answers to a series of questionnaires sent out to members of the Association in 1911 showed that they were already considered "an integral part of general education"), but also because they believed the sheer inflexibility of the group system would strangle initiative and experiment in teaching. Year after year from 1918 to 1951

(*By permission of The Times Educational Supplement*)

when the School Certificate was replaced by the General Certificate of Education they proposed amendments with steady, and to the Board no doubt maddening, persistence. In 1926 they suggested that five passes in subjects taken from Group One and *any* two other groups, should give a certificate but the Board apparently shared the view of university representatives on the Secondary Schools Examination Council that the "group system" was "not in need of alteration." So the arguments flew back and forth for another ten years, with other teachers' associations joining in, until in 1936 the university representation on the Council was halved and the next year the original suggestion of the Association was adopted in its entirety.

The Association did more than oppose restrictive regulations in examinations. It put forward other ideas which were well in advance of the time and which at first received only very luke-warm support outside its ranks. It favoured a "subject" examination, instead of the School Certificate, in which a candidate should not "pass or fail" in the examination as a whole but receive a certificate recording passes in individual subjects. This is now universal practice. It canvassed the possibility of continuous assessment as an aid if not a complete substitute for a once-and-for-all examination, a method which now forty years later has been fully accepted and is used at all levels from school to university. Individual head mistresses experimented with courses which were not examined at all and later, when the GCE took the place of the School Certificate, with the by-passing of Ordinary level. And long before "general subjects in the sixth form" became fashionable they had established them in their schools, though without the "carrot" of an examination which later in boys' schools was found to be the only certain guarantee of acceptability. These courses were given a chapter to themselves in the Crowther *Report on the Education of the 15- to 18-year-old*, and the conclusion was that they were a source of strength to the schools, and to follow them would be as good for boys as for girls.

Girls' schools have never been bound by the idea of responsibility vested only in a small élite of prefects and games captains, and up and down the country there developed methods of achieving responsible freedom so that children of all ages became accustomed to genuine self-government. The result was a variety of democratic devices, form committees, school councils, election of school officers, control of societies, all giving experience of what is known as "participation," now loudly demanded where it has not already become a matter of course.

Throughout this period the vigour of the secondary schools and the value of the education they gave was constantly evident. Forty-one years after the Act which had created so many of them the Norwood Report described their products as "enterprising, adaptable, and capable of meeting . . . the very special demands made in new developments of applied science and of linguistic study." The success of the schools stimulated the demand for more, and the question was being constantly asked "Why must these opportunities be restricted to so few?' For the grammar schools catered for only a tiny minority and though "an educational ladder had been provided," as G.A. Lowndes wrote in *The Silent Social Revolution*, "it was still a steep one and several rungs were missing." The odds against a child from an elementary school gaining a free place in a secondary one had shortened from 270 to one in 1894 to ten to one in 1935, but the vast majority had still only what the elementary schools could give them and this, in spite of devoted and often very skilful teaching, was severely limited by tradition and by inadequate facilities. There had been development but little concrete change, and so demand grew for further extension and more opportunities. It came from many quarters as it had come in 1902; from nearly all sections of the teaching profession, from politicians—in 1916 the Labour Party had adopted the slogan "Secondary Education for All"—and from writers like R.H. Tawney, who produced a best-seller with the same title. Articulate parents, both those who had themselves attended secondary schools and those who had not but who recognized the value of what they gave, now clamoured for the same or better opportunities for their children. The influence of movements like the Workers' Educational Association, and the University Extension courses steadily increased. In 1926 the Hadow Report on the *Education of the Adolescent* recommended post-primary education for all children after the age of eleven and proposed the raising of the leaving age to fifteen by

1932. This last proposal was not implemented. The severe depression of 1931 forced new economies on education and by the time it was again recommended the Second World War had engulfed the nation.

Throughout the 'twenties and 'thirties the Association of Head Mistresses was deeply involved in inquiries, discussions and committees. It had representatives on the Secondary Schools Examination Council, the two Hadow Committees and the Spens Committee. It formulated its own policies for the future, not in limited or parochial terms but in bold perspectives. In 1937 the theme of the annual Conference was "Education and Society," in 1938 "Education and the State." At the first Muriel Davies spoke. She was a remarkable person and a peerless teacher whose literature lessons made an indelible mark on her pupils and whose love of poetry opened new worlds to them. She used to bicycle through London to meetings with a rucksack on her back containing among other things her knitting, for she had an adopted family of five for whom she knitted ceaselessly. Dedicated to the idea of a classless society, she made a plea for an educational system which she believed would produce it, not "one built up on class distinction" as in her view the English system was, but on "multi-bias" secondary schools where a child would enter a course best suited to his capacity, with no difference between rich and poor. This was strong meat, certain to arouse opposition, and a heated debate followed, though not by any means a one-sided one. In 1938 Dorothy de Zouche rejected the idea of uniformity immediately enforced. She insisted that the change to truly democratic education would come bit by bit: "In a series, it may be, of lurches, of zig-zags from right to left and back again, ground is gained." At the same Conference accounts were given, and discussed, of the educational systems of Russia, by Sir Bernard Pares and Mrs Beatrice King, and of Germany by Doctor Wilmsen, and this was a sign of the prevailing readiness to examine other patterns and methods of education with interest and self-criticism, in spite of the growing darkness on the world's horizons.

Then in 1939, with the declaration of war, theory and planning went by the board and emergency took over. The situation which faced the nation was quite unlike that of

1914-18 and it had direct and catastrophic effects on education. These first stemmed from evacuation and those extraordinary first four days in September 1939 when there took place what Chuter Ede, Parliamentary Secretary for Education, later called

HABERDASHERS' ASKE'S SCHOOL,

WEST ACTON, W.3.

27th September 1938.

Dear Sir or Madam,

The School Governors have decided that should a state of emergency be declared by the Government they will close the school and avail themselves of the Government scheme for evacuating children from this area. Children will be sent away in parties of ten under the care of their mistresses or some other responsible person. Further details I shall be glad to supply at 7 p.m. this evening and 8.30 a.m. tomorrow morning.

At the appointed time children to be evacuated will be instructed to assemble at school with:

a) Hand luggage.
b) Mackintosh or coat.
c) Blanket.
d) One day's food.

All these should be kept in readiness.

Will you kindly answer on the enclosed slip whether you wish your child to be evacuated with the school and return the paper at once?

Yours very truly,

(Signed) D. W. SPRULES.

Evacuation. The letter sent in September 1938 to the parents of pupils at a London School.
(By permission of the Governors of Haberdashers' Aske's Acton School)

"the most remarkable movement of civil population ever recorded in history" in the course of which 750,000 children and their teachers were moved from London and the great industrial centres to safer areas.

This great achievement had its dark, its comic and its serious sides. It revealed with startling clearness some of the black spots of English social life; it made plain the fact that "one half of England had no idea how the other half lived"; it drew forth high praise of the work of teachers. It revealed ludicrous contradictions and shortcomings in bureaucratic procedure, as for instance when teachers were allowed five shillings a day for their keep and civil servants twenty-one shillings, and when the Treasury produced the fatuous sum of £1 per 200 for those children who were in need of warm clothing and sound shoes. There were scores of stories told about the whole episode and violent speeches in Parliament attempting to apportion blame for mistakes. Many vivid descriptive passages can be found in the records of the schools.

One hundred and eighty girls' schools whose head mistresses belonged to the Association were evacuated, and an almost equal number shared their premises with others. Their experiences were very varied. One northern school arrived in a rural area where they found five others in possession and not a billet to be had. Its determined head mistress commandeered the buses which had brought them and were about to return, and drove round the area until an unoccupied zone was found into which she decanted her pupils and staff. Another school found itself dispersed over thirteen villages with public transport between only three of them. Teaching conditions were often unspeakably difficult, as in the school where Art was taught in "a vast shack of corrugated iron and cement which had once been a garage," where icicles hung from the roof in cold weather and glutinous layers of oil had to be scraped from the floor before work could begin. Some were luckier than others and worked in such places as "the cricket pavilion ... surprisingly warm and comfortable with long wooden tables and faded photographs of Victorian teams." But always the teaching went on with extraordinary dedication and cheerful improvisation.

Those who were billeted in stately homes had some odd

...when the Treasury produced the fatuous sum of £1 per 200 for those children who were in need of warm clothing and sound shoes
(Drawing by David Lamb)

experiences. One school occupied the servants' quarters, shut off from the rest of the house by green baize doors, and a range of rooms over the stables, smelling strongly of hay. Only after arduous negotiations was the billiard-room handed over as a class-room. Here irreverent schoolgirls hung their satchels round the necks of the stuffed stags adorning the walls, left *Latin for Today* lying next to *My Experiences in the Hunting Field* and tattered French grammars on top of an uncut copy of *Fifty Years at Eton*. Of course in most instances there was an immediate response of generous welcome and great practical kindness to the migrant schools and lasting links and permanent friendships were formed. But there were bound to be cases of less understanding and some friction, especially over shared premises, and cases of schools carefully kept apart in all activities. "The Collegiate staff, I rather think, tried to pretend we were not there, and there was no fraternization." One school, whose refuge turned out to be less safe than expected, suffered a severe incendiary raid soon after it arrived. The girls took to the cellars. So did the household of the owner including the elderly dowager and her maid, who were settled in a corner behind a screen. When the all-clear sounded and she picked her way among the girls on the floor she was heard to ask her maid in penetrating tones, "Bennett, *who* are all these people?"

Many of the experiences, though strange, were also enriching. The schools, pupils, staff and heads, learned to share in the daily lives of other quite different communities and families. City-bred girls had a taste of life in the country, the village, or the small town. There grew up a far greater understanding and informality between teachers and pupils and teachers and parents as they wrestled together with problems, improvised everyday necessaries, reduced confusion to order and somehow carried on the essential business of education. For long periods the school had to replace the home, albeit often with wonderful help from the families who "billeted" children, and heads and staff had to act as substitutes for parents. The heads of all schools, whether evacuated or not, were required to undertake new and often exacting responsibilities, coping with the harassed and the homesick, with ministries, committees and authorities, with a sea of regulations and restrictions of every kind. A London School evacuated to Wales had to deal with the

Carmarthenshire Education Committee and the Llanelly Education Committee, the Board of Education in London and its
Welsh Department in Cardiff, the Ministry of Health, the Welsh
Board of Health, the London County Council and its office in
Cardiff, the authorities of a church who had lent a crypt and
the governing body of the school. "The organization of our life
was always complicated by the fact that we served many
masters," wrote the head mistress. "Often we did not know till
we had done the wrong thing who it was we ought to have
asked. Sometimes we had to do first and ask afterwards for
there are times when people matter more than filling in the
right form in triplicate." So head mistresses, along with the
unalterably personal side of their work in school, carried also
the task of tackling official, impersonal problems not always
capable of solution. "I am directed to refer you to the following
official publications . . ." ran the stately answer to a request for
immediate information about the release of air-raid shelters
after the fall of France, but the publications proved to deal with
"The Stretcher Problem" and "The Use of Rationed Foods in
War Time," and the whole correspondence had to begin again.

With members dispersed and under acute pressure, with
London and other cities under enemy attack, with scarcity of
paper and erratic posts, it was not easy to maintain any of the
functions of the Association. Yet this was done, as the records
show. Contact with individual members was kept going and help
with their problems made available. The Executive committee
continued to carry out an extraordinary amount of work.
Meetings with the Joint Four (the abbreviated title of the joint
executive committee of four Secondary Associations, Assistant
Mistresses, Assistant Masters, Head Masters and Head Mistresses)
went on regularly; deputations or individuals visited the
Ministries of Education, of Health, of Labour and of Pensions.
Correspondence continued with the Universities, Training Colleges, Local Authorities, the Association of Hospital Matrons,
the National Union of Teachers, the National Union of
Students, and, not surprisingly, with the Secondary Schools
Examinations Council. All this went on regardless of the fact
that the headquarters of the Association at 29 Gordon Square
were bombed and the office had to move out of London. For a
time, however, it was found impossible even for head mistresses

to organize major conferences and from 1939 to 1942 annual general meetings only were held for such members as could get to them. Yet, in spite of everything, continuity was preserved and communication never ceased.

It is a remarkable thing that in the midst of all the perils and preoccupations of war, the tide of educational thought at this time, far from ebbing, flowed more strongly than ever, in the Association and all other teachers' associations, in the minds of statesmen and politicians, and among the public at large. Yet perhaps this was natural, because more and more the schools were coming to be seen as part of the community, and education as an essential preparation for democratic living. This was not only owing to the shocks sustained by the nation through the experiences of the war, but to the hopes of a better order of society when the conflict ended. A letter to *The Times* in 1940 headed "Foundations of Peace" and signed by the Archbishops of Canterbury and York, the Roman Catholic Archbishop of Westminster and the Moderator of the Free Church Federal Council, urged the provision of equal opportunities for every child to develop his particular capacities—words which were to grow so familiar as to become a cliché. With the appointment of R.A. Butler as President of the Board of Education in July 1941 things were bound to move. He was the third in that office in three years but, in his own words, "had always looked forward to going to the Board of Education." Now he was given the "opportunity to harness to the educational system the wartime urge for social reform and greater equality."

A month earlier Butler's predecessor had issued a memorandum on *Education after the War*—soon to be known from the colour of its binding as "The Green Book"—in which the aspirations of the Board for post-war education were set out. Secondary education should be free for all children from the age of eleven. Britain after the war must be educationally one nation, so there must be provision for every kind of talent and ability, with opportunities for some form of further education after school in County Colleges. The other side of the proposals concerned the hitherto intractable religious question and the "dual system" of provided and non-provided schools, which was to demand long and delicate negotiations for its solution.

The Green Book was labelled "Strictly confidential" and there were extraordinary omissions from the list of those permitted to see it—the editor of *The Times Educational Supplement* being one of them—but it was issued "in such a blaze of secrecy" that it roused immediate interest in all quarters, including those "to whom the President of the Board of Education decided in his wisdom *not* to make known its contents"! Within six months the Association of Head Mistresses in company with the other constituent members of the Joint Four, sent an agreed memorandum to the Board welcoming the main proposals while reserving the right to add a separate memorandum from the particular viewpoint of head mistresses. This in fact was drawn up and sent three months later after the annual Conference of the Association at Malvern Girls' College in April 1942.

But the Association had certainly not waited till 1942 before considering educational reconstruction. It had been constantly discussed in the executive committee and already in 1941, before the Green Book appeared, the subject of speeches at the Annual General Meeting had been "A Post-War Educational Policy." Clearly too there was basic agreement on certain principles in spite of some notes of caution. One of these came from Mary Clarke, who argued that a united teaching profession (not even now after thirty years a reality) should precede a national system of education; but on the other hand she boldly recommended, as desirable reforms, co-education after the School Certificate stage, the merging of university departments of education with training colleges, and at least three years training for teachers. There was also support—foreshadowing one of the recommendations of the Plowden report—for a break in schooling at thirteen instead of eleven, as well as for "multi-bias" schools. These were some of the preliminaries. It was at Malvern in 1942 that the major issues of post-war education were faced, and policy decided.

This was the first full Annual Conference held by the Association since the outbreak of war. It was an historic occasion, when immediate trials and problems were disregarded and head mistresses addressed themselves to the "Fundamentals in Education for English Democracy." It was recognized from the beginning, and the President, Dorothy de Zouche, made it abundantly clear in her address to the Conference, that there was in the Association a united conviction of the need for a genuinely democratic system of education, "a corporate and an individual desire that the schools in which we serve shall as fully and truly as possible serve the community." On this basis and after far-ranging discussion the following main resolutions were passed: "That in the opinion of this Association (*a*) the whole educational system of the country should embody the principles of democracy: (*b*) that no financial or social barrier should therefore prevent any child from receiving the education best suited to his needs and abilities; (*c*,1) that no fees should be charged for tuition in secondary schools in receipt of public money; (*c*,2) that any financial loss incurred by those schools ... which are not maintained or aided by a local authority should be made good from public funds until such time as those schools may be included in the general scheme of education." This last conservative clause left open the way for continuation of public and independent schools at least for a time, but it evoked a radical amendment from Muriel Davies to the effect that "for the building up of a democratic society it is essential that all schools should offer education without fees and should come within the national system" and "that private, public, proprietary, and independent schools should be abolished or incorporated in the national system." Muriel Davies and those who supported her foresaw an even sharper cleavage between the education of the poorer and the richer if the independent sector remained entrenched, and a continuation of a dangerous divisiveness, and who would say that they were wrong in fearing this? There tends still to circulate a hoary traditional image of head mistresses as ultra-conservative, and firmly wedded to neat tailor-made suits and the *status quo*; but if this were true then surely at this moment such a revolutionary amendment would have been heavily defeated. In fact it was lost only by 117 votes to 172. It was replaced by a cautious compromise "that some way should be found of bringing the independent schools into closer relationship with the national system" but the vote was an indication of views strongly held by many. At the time Dorothy Brock and Emmeline Tanner were both members of the Fleming Committee which published in 1944 its *Report on the Public Schools and the General Educational System.* A sincere attempt was made to find a means of closer association between the two sections but little or nothing came of it. Malvern marked a new stage in the history of the Association. In spite of genuine differences of opinion it achieved a joint declaration of principles, redefined its philosophy and aligned itself with forward thinking for the new world ahead.

In the early days the pioneers had asked themselves what they must assert as educators and head mistresses and what, in time, they might have to surrender. Their successors had already surrendered a marked social and intellectual exclusiveness and an almost regal freedom of the head mistress from interference by an outside authority. What they were rapidly losing was the unhurried pace of school life, and a curriculum not yet endangered by subject demands and examination requirements. What they continued to assert was a belief in quality and freedom, a concern for the individual child as a whole person, "the immutable centre of all educational systems," and an intention to serve the community of which the school was a part. With these fundamental assertions they moved into the post-war period.

Chapter 7

Secondary education for all

The Education Act became law in August 1944. Over the whole of the three years since the appearance of the Green Book its provisions had been the subject of passionate interest and long discussion, and reports, pamphlets, and memoranda had poured into the Board of Education from every conceivable body either directly or remotely concerned with education, and from individuals as well. Its passage through Parliament after this prolonged period of preparation and negotiation took only thirty-four days compared with fifty-three for the much shorter Act of 1902, but this swift passage did not indicate any indifference in either Lords or Commons, but rather the reverse, a general determination that the Bill should become law. The whole debate was at a very high level, marked by enthusiasm and earnestness, and many remarkable speeches were made. "The time was ripe," as Butler himself said. This was the first of the great pieces of social reconstruction for which, after five years of war, the whole nation longed and even those who criticized certain sections of it did not oppose its underlying principles, many of which had indeed been canvassed long before the Second World War. Nearly every speaker therefore warmly welcomed the main provisions and critics were often disarmed by the patent sincerity of R.A. Butler and Chuter Ede, his Parliamentary Secretary, and by their willingness patiently to consider criticisms and proposals for amendment. Even Winston Churchill, whose views on education Butler later described as "decidedly idiosyncratic" and who in 1941 had firmly discouraged any idea of introducing a new Education Act, saying that Butler's main task ought to be "to get the schools working as well as possible under all the difficulties," sent a generous telegram of congratulation when, despite his own reservations, that Act did in fact become law. "Pray accept my congratulations. You have added a notable Act to the Statute book, and won a lasting place in the history of British education." Notable the Act certainly was and so it remains, and all the delays, the problems, and the frustrations and all the changes of viewpoints of the thirty years since its passing must never be allowed to obscure that fact.

It was a massive piece of legislation of 122 clauses and 8 schedules and all its sections need not be described here. The most momentous of its provisions were:

1. The raising of the school-leaving age to fifteen and secondary education for all "according to age, aptitude and ability."

2. The sweeping away of the old division between element-ary and secondary education and its replacement by "a continuous process conducted in three stages, primary, secondary and further education."

3. The abolition of fees in all state secondary schools.

The Association of Head Mistresses, having urged all three of these reforms at intervals since 1924, warmly welcomed them, though, with a rather naïve underestimate of the sheer impossibility of housing the extra numbers involved, they openly stated their disappointment that the leaving age was not to be sixteen! They were also dismayed at the failure to abolish fees in all secondary schools receiving grants of public money whether from local authorities or directly from the Treasury. Agnes Catnach at the Conference in 1943 had spoken of the "peculiar joy and pride of this Association that it has united within itself every kind of girls' secondary school, new and old, state-provided or independent"; but she went on prophetically to say, "The new Education Act will probably split the ranks of our present secondary schools on the question of fees, and raise unnatural divisions among us." She was right; the divisions appeared and, though they did not destroy the unity of the Association, produced inevitable tensions within it.

Even in a time of peace and affluence the process of

implementing the great measure of reconstruction and inno-
vation would have taken a long time—R.A. Butler himself
expected it to need a generation—and now after that generation
the process is, to some extent, still incomplete. But in 1944,
nearing the end of an exhausting war and with every kind of
shortage and of restriction on supplies and manpower, the time
was neither peaceful nor affluent. Certainly teachers, for all
their welcome and enthusiasm, had no illusions about the
enormous task that lay ahead of them before "secondary
education for all" could become reality. "The captains and the
kings depart—the teachers remain"; again it is Agnes Catnach
speaking in 1943, and the head mistresses who listened had a
fair idea of what that meant.

The planning of education for the post-war world had been
conceived on bold and generous lines, but now all the "new
thinking for new times" must continue alongside the arduous
day-to-day labours and against a background of the disruption
caused by the war. However glorious the thought that "the true
measure of nations is what they can do when they are tired" the
reality was tough rather than glorious, and produced a feeling of
being "hedged round by difficulties rather than led into a
promised land."

While head mistresses did not lose their vision or their nerve,
they were bound to take stock of the difficulties, and at the
Conference in 1945 the President, Sybil Smith (King Edward's
High School, Birmingham) made some of them explicit. She was
speaking at a moment when after six years of war most of her
audience were tired; when, though hostilities had ended in
Europe, they had not ceased everywhere; when only the
summer before girls in London schools had written their
examination papers in air-raid shelters because of V-bomb
attacks. To say, as she did, that "the Act comes into operation
at an extraordinarily unpromising time" was to make an
understatement. She spoke of the destruction of buildings. In
fact one-fifth of all the schools in the country had been made
totally useless through enemy action and another fifth had been
commandeered for other purposes, Air raid precaution posts,
fire-stations, rest-centres, military headquarters or Government
departments, and were released only very slowly and after stern
battles. In all 151,000 school places had been lost and to raise

the school-leaving age to fifteen, which was done in 1947, not only had these lost places to be replaced but 300,000 new ones provided. Sybil Smith went on to speak of the shortage of teachers, acute even before the war, but now desperate, and aggravated every week by the very natural disappearance of those married women who had come in during the war to help, and of the veterans who had gone staunchly on well after retirement age and now desired a well-earned relief. She mentioned too the scarcity of basic equipment, materials, and especially books. It is easy to forget these shortages in the comparative affluence of 1974; to forget that there was strict rationing not only of clothes, tea, sugar, cheese, bread, potatoes, fats, eggs, meat, but also of petrol and paper, and how all this could affect both strength and spirits; to forget that many head mistresses had only just ceased to be fire-watchers by night, and by day perhaps caretakers, organizers of pig-buckets (for waste food) and billeting officers, running the school with one hand and with the other possibly giving help in the kitchen when dinners were threatened by a hopelessly inadequate domestic staff that sometimes changed every week!

One of the first things the Association had to decide was whether to open its membership to the head mistresses of those girls' schools which as the result of the Act had suddenly, at the moment of the Royal Assent, become "secondary." There were about nine hundred of these and through 1944 and 1945 the question was debated long and carefully "whether the Association was to remain an association of head mistresses of grammar schools only, or whether membership was to be extended to the heads of modern and technical schools." It was not a decision to be taken lightly and there were two main anxieties in the minds of members. They feared the loss of close contacts and easy intimate discussion which might result from a sudden increase in numbers. The old cosy days when fifty or sixty members were thought an excessively large number were long past and there were now 640, but it seemed possible that this number might easily double. They feared too a change in the character of the Association through a flood of new members from schools many of which, as it was bluntly but truthfully said, "were secondary only in name." Both fears were strong and justified (the second at any rate was strong enough among head masters to make them hesitate for another year before extending the membership of their association), and opinion was carefully tested by a letter from the President sent to every member asking for her views, followed by a vote taken at the Conference in June 1945. This was another vital moment in the life of the Association and a strange parallel with the position in 1902. Then it had rejected a position of exclusiveness; now for the second time, and in spite of reservations and fears, its members rejected by a large majority the dangerous, perhaps the fatal, step of cutting themselves off from the mainstream of education. They passed a resolution, proposed by Emmeline Tanner, "that this Association welcomes to its membership head mistresses of the new secondary schools"—schools which she described as "with traditions still to be made and standards differing in character but not, we hope and believe, in quality from our own." She was over-optimistic; there proved to be enormous differences in standards. Thirty years later the head mistress of a secondary modern school wrote, "I think, perhaps, that in welcoming members from the whole secondary field you made a decision as important for our generation as did the Beales, the Busses and the Burstalls for theirs."

The establishment and maintenance of quality in education had been from the first a positive obsession with the Association of Head Mistresses. Initially they had limited this to a narrow field when they asserted the potential capabilities of girls compared with those of boys. They then extended the search for quality beyond the traditional grammar school curriculum into a much wider range of subjects and activities, art, music, drama and the like; then, after 1902, into a greater number and variety of schools, in fact into a new section of society. No one could challenge the value of this quest and it was something that Michael Sadler had recognized when he spoke, in 1905 to the North of England Conference on Education, of the spirit in the best girls' schools as being "one of the gifts of England to the modern conception of education, easy to preserve as the exclusive social possession of a few but only to be fully used when it spread slowly from one school to another till it has leavened the whole."

Now in the post-war period this same quest for quality was

always to the forefront in the mind of the Association, the first call on the energies of its members and their staffs. The results of the war on education had been profound and varied. On the credit side were the closer bonds of understanding between teachers and pupils, and between teachers and parents, challenged perhaps today as not yet close or adequate enough, but real none the less. There was the broader outlook of adolescents and their greater independence and self-reliance. There were the more flexible methods of teaching which had stemmed from enforced improvisation. On the debit side was the falling-off of concentration, the decline in educational standards and sometimes in enthusiasm, and the sheer loss of schooling by some children; for in 1941, half-way through the war, fourteen per cent of children of secondary age and twenty-seven per cent of primary were receiving no education at all. There was much to do to overcome these losses. In the established schools head mistresses and staff alike were bent on the recovery of standards and their thoughts and energies absorbed in making good the loss in the education of the children in schools which had been evacuated, dispersed, or temporarily closed, which had shared premises or been restricted and starved of resources in countless other ways.

In the new secondary schools, modern and technical, the immensely responsible task of building them up was even more formidable, especially as many of them, in addition to all other problems, had to establish themselves fully in the public esteem. If some of them attempted to do this simply by imitating the grammar schools, most of them did not, but sought to remain free of the stranglehold of the grammar school curriculum which was unrelated to the needs of the majority of their pupils but which was fixed in the public's mind as the model of what a secondary school should offer. Perhaps the recognition that they must be free to experiment, to develop in their own way and not be identified with established patterns was one of the reasons why head mistresses in those modern and technical schools which had women in charge of them did not rush to join the Association. Besides this many of them preferred the appeal of a larger professional association and yet others undoubtedly harboured an image of head mistresses as academically and socially exclusive! Those who, in steadily growing numbers, did become members were many of them young, most of them had been educated in the grammar schools, and some had taught in them. They were often newly appointed, enthusiastic and ready to experiment; they felt themselves again to be pioneers and they were a fertilizing influence in the Association. In their turn they were often glad to feel that an experienced, and by now an influential, body was behind them, speaking for the particular needs of girls at the secondary stage and ready to support them in difficulties. There were pockets of reaction and coolness certainly, and some lofty head mistresses in grammar schools seemed unaware of the existence of those in modern schools, but what might appear to be "starch and snobbery" to the sensitive was in reality only an

'*Well, as we're doing away with gym slips for the Sixth Form, I thought to myself, "Why not?"*'

(By permission of The Manchester Evening News)

initial lack of understanding. For the most part there was a warm welcome for the new colleagues and a genuine interest in—if not always a complete understanding of—their problems, both educational and social, which were often a healthy eye-opener for those who had not yet met them. "The executive committee of the Association presented the most forward-looking, the most liberal and the most positively friendly group of grammar school heads, but that welcoming attitude was not universal," wrote one head mistress of a modern school. Nevertheless many of them found it "a refreshment at meetings and conferences to get into an atmosphere where educational values were more important than salaries and dinner duties," and a practical help to know "what amenities the selective schools had, what to ask for, and how to cope with obstructive authorities"!

Today it may seem that in 1944 too many head mistresses blindly accepted the selective system with its pattern either of grammar, technical and modern schools, or of only grammar and modern, which, except in a few areas, became the usual one for the organization of secondary education. But two things must be said if not in justification at least in explanation. One is the absorption already mentioned, in restoring standards in the schools they served, as well as in the multiplicity of calls which were increasingly made on their time and energy. The other is the fact that before the war the Association had already discussed at length—albeit often with incomplete understanding and sympathy—the idea of multi-bias or comprehensive schools and at their best many members must have doubted whether "the fullest possible educational opportunities could be extended to all the nation's children" in any other context. But while some pursued the idea with a greater sense of conviction and immediacy, the majority were content to be part of the social context in which they found themselves and to do the work which lay under their hands in the framework provided; content not to be prophets, to shut their eyes to the fact that in the tripartite system of grammar, modern and technical schools there might be planted the seeds of future discontent. Yet, while this is true, it is also true that the tripartite organization was an essential step toward democratic education. No other was generally practicable at the time.

After quality and high standards the Association had, from the first, been concerned with freedom and individuality. Thring said that the girls' schools had not been bound by "the rigid moulds of the past" in framing the curriculum but had experimented freely in subjects and content. Not having copied only the patterns of the middle ages, the schools were markedly individual and diverse. But diversity is always administratively inconvenient and when the grammar schools joined the primary, modern, and technical schools in the "continuous process conducted in three stages" under a single Code of Regulations, the bureaucratic shoe which had pinched in some places after 1902 now tended to be much more uncomfortable. Some authorities, of course, set to work to implement the Act swiftly and in a truly liberal spirit and in real partnership with their teachers, but others seemed to suffer from such an excess of administrative zeal that machinery became an end in itself, and from such a passion for tidiness that their aim was uniformity based on restriction rather than a realization of the vast opportunities of the Act. Of these John Wolfenden, then Vice-Chancellor of Reading University, wrote, "Now and then they seem—and this is the most terrible thing—to be by temperament the enemies, instead of the friends, of their teachers." So head mistresses often found themselves subjected on a scale greater than they had known to irritating restraints which were usually the disagreeable remnants of the old regulations for elementary schools and were particularly galling to professional people who had for long managed schools successfully without trivial interference. In some areas time-sheets were again demanded; leave of absence for attending educational conferences in term was refused unless pay was forfeited, even as late as 1970; school visits to museums, theatres, and field courses, formerly arranged as a matter of course, were not allowed without permission in writing from an inspector; holidays were reduced below the maximum permitted, and this hit the maintained grammar schools hard and widened the division between them and schools receiving direct grant. The fortuitous imposition of burdens and restrictions, many of them petty in themselves, often strained relationships between the secondary schools and the local authorities, and in some places have not even now entirely disappeared. Worst of all many head mistresses who before 1944 had retained the freedom of appointing assistant teachers to their schools now found themselves again subjected to the survival of the old elementary code and denied this responsibility. The policy of appointing assistant staff without reference to the head, and dealing them out "like cards from a pack" to the secondary schools, so detested after 1902, was again used by some of the worst authorities and again repudiated as illiberal and unsound, yet it is still followed by some intransigent authorities in spite of all professional pressure. As late as 1970 Beryl Williams (Reigate County School) castigated in her presidential speech "those authorities which do not entrust the head with any power to select staff. I know of two occasions this year," she said, "where new appointments were made without the head being consulted at all; she had not even seen the candidates and one of them was to be her deputy!" The Association vigorously resisted all this strait-jacketing. Alone or in company with colleagues in other associations it made direct approaches to local authorities and to the Minister. Above all it continually urged that teachers should have direct representation on Education Committees in every area. A list recently drawn up of teacher representation over the whole country shows what great progress in this has been made since 1944; it also shows, less happily, that in a few backwoods the struggle still continues.

It was of course inescapable that the tremendous enlargement of the field of secondary education after 1944, if that education was to be secondary in anything more than name, would present problems and anxieties that called for stout hearts as well as fine adjustments. The Association never wavered in its enthusiasm for the Act. It recorded many times its hope that the result would be a levelling-up of all schools; but its members would have been less than human and quite unrealistic if they had not also had fears that it might be "a levelling down not to the worst standards of the past but to something less good than the best of the present." Were those fears justified? Even now after thirty years of "Secondary Education for All" it would be hazardous to make any final assessment of the result on standards, especially when so much energy and money has at times been deflected from education to organization, and further it would be dishonest to pretend that in some ways and some areas there has not been a falling-off from the best standards existing before 1944, or a failure to reach them. One obvious practical reason for this is that an expansion of education greater than any known before in this country has coincided with a chronic shortage of money aggravated by recurrent economic crises. Even if resources had been unlimited the enormous task of putting in practice the Butler Act could hardly have come about without some checks to standards. But resources have not been unlimited, or steadily and predictably forthcoming, nor have they always been evenly distributed. There has been the further complication of a growth of nearly four million in the school population, partly due to rising birth-rates and partly to voluntary staying on in school beyond the statutory leaving-age. All this has happened in a period which began at the end of a costly war which shook society to its roots, disrupted its education, and caused acute shortage of buildings, equipment and teachers, shortages which had to be made good at the same time as massive new plans were being launched.

There has been a great escalation of public spending on schools, from £107 million in 1947 to £814 million in 1967, and to £1,475 million in 1972. But these monies have all along been affected by rising costs and the diminishing purchasing power of the pound. We know only too well that "the pound in your pocket" buys far fewer household goods for the family than it did ten or twenty years ago. It also buys fewer bricks and less mortar for school buildings and fewer of the tools of education. The cost of reconstruction has been heavy, the recovery from wartime damage and scarcity slower than many people had hoped, and the raising of the school-leaving age twice has meant that "roofs over heads" have had to be put before refinements.

It has always been possible for those who were in charge of grammar schools to point to their obvious needs which were only slowly and sometimes never satisfied. Head mistresses were impatient with delay and not content to wait a moment longer than absolutely necessary for what they wanted. Reports of meetings at executive and at branch level were full of efforts to speed up supplies of books, science equipment and desks, of anxiety about space for increasing numbers, about "floating" forms that had no base because all rooms were occupied, and about inadequate provision of specialist accommodation. Many schools had plans drawn up in the 'fifties for new accommodation for growing sixth forms only to have them set aside year after year because other schools had still more urgent needs, such as indoor lavatories or the basic necessities for teaching science. It is easy to understand frustration in such cases, less easy now to be sympathetic to those swift requests, when the war ended, to the Ministry of Supply for a better flow of school hats!

But of course the grammar schools, however much they might complain, had a head start over the "new" secondary schools. The majority of modern schools were often housed in their old elementary school premises, unchanged except in name, built in a repellent style of architecture, inflexible, and unmodernized, and had not only to catch up on their wartime losses and hope for adaptations, but acquire what many of them had never had. "Modern schools were often without libraries, laboratories, gymnasiums and changing rooms," wrote the head mistress of one, and she might have added playing fields, music provision and much of the equipment necessary for functioning as secondary schools. "Equipment in the secondary sense was entirely absent" was the experience of a school in the north, and in that particular school no child had a book to herself in class. The Association was quickly alive to the problems of its new members. In March 1945 the first of a number of letters went to the Minister asking for special consideration to be given to them so that the new secondary schools should have "amenities and opportunities approaching as nearly as possible to those of the best of the existing schools. This is a matter of first importance if they are to be given a chance of establishing a sense of their value and prestige in the mind of the public." But it was the local authorities, not the Ministry, that needed to be urged. While some were bold and generous and gave priority where it was really needed, others were tardy and cheese-paring, and others frankly discriminated in favour of their selective schools. Levelling-up "to the best" was very slow in some places, and in some it was never achieved. The idea seemed to linger that it was quite proper to provide a shorter, cheaper form of education for children who at eleven plus appeared to be less able than others.

Yet over the country as a whole a prodigious amount has been achieved since 1944. The programme of building, much of it for secondary schools, which began with what the Ministry, in a revealing phrase, referred to as "Hutting Operations" in its Report of 1947, often seemed to proceed by fits and starts, or with wearisome delays, but it resulted in 7,200 new schools by 1967 and 11,740 by 1971, spacious, airy and superbly equipped. Gradually a mass of educational tools from simple basic necessities to sophisticated· modern equipment for language and science teaching, television and physical education has found its way into schools of every type.

But there has been one shortage, most obstinate of all and most inimical to quality in education which has been much more slowly remedied—the shortage of teachers. In 1944 the situation was bleak; it was to grow bleaker still. During the war recruitment had been almost at a standstill; some training colleges had been closed, and the trickle of teachers coming out of the others and from the universities was totally inadequate. It was hoped that 200,000 teachers might return to the schools from active service but it was also calculated that at least 12,000 would be lost each year through normal wastage. As only 6,000 to 7,000 new teachers would reach the schools from training college and university departments of education, a short-fall of about 6,000 seemed inevitable, unless the numbers recruited and trained could be increased. The supply of teachers, fundamental at any time and crucial to the realization of secondary education for all, had been inadequate before but never quite so precarious.

Head mistresses for a hundred years have been insistent on the need for well-qualified teachers. Originally it was only by qualifying that they became professionally accepted and respectable, and to them "qualified" has always meant—and still means—properly trained for the job, not simply fed with tribal lore passed down through the generations. With almost monotonous regularity from 1906 onwards the training of teachers appears as the subject for conferences and discussions among themselves or with universities and training colleges. At times they admitted to disappointment either with the quality of training or the attitude of graduates towards it. Now with history repeating itself more dangerously than ever before, they braced themselves for new exertion and campaigning. Some members took part at the very end of the war in the preparations of the Emergency Training Scheme for giving a short intensive course in fifty temporary colleges to men and women released from war service. Some at very short notice— for the scheme was hurriedly improvised—and in spite of their own acute difficulties, released some of their best staff to become lecturers in the Emergency colleges. But the 33,000 teachers trained under this scheme made small impact in the secondary schools and the Ministry's massive programme of expansion in the permanent colleges took a very long time to get under way and even longer to produce results. Recruitment of graduates was sparse, the wastage rate rose steadily— particularly among women—the growing numbers of children, bluntly called as "the Bulge," inexorably moved into and through the schools. The position in girls' schools worsened alarmingly. They were largely, though by no means entirely, dependent on women teachers, and of these marriage and wider job opportunities took heavy toll. The scarcity was predictably worse in some areas and some subjects. Head mistresses in unattractive urban areas, especially when trying to appoint mathematics or science teachers, lived in a chronic state of anxiety, while the fortunate who worked in more favoured places such as university towns lost little sleep. Regularly in the years 1947 to 1968 the Association sent out questionnaires on staffing to all its members and the returns built up into a grim recital of shortages, punctuated with notes of near despair, "No application" or, in the language of the hunt, "Tracked down an applicant" and "One applicant was seized."

In 1960 the President, Nonita Glenday (Clifton High School), spoke at the Conference about the gravity of the situation and made it clear that the tremendous opportunities in education were overshadowed by the persistent shortage of teachers. She pressed home her argument with examples drawn from the answers to these annual questionnaires. She urged the need for greater official activity from the Ministry, and from all groups and individuals who could influence and encourage recruitment.

The efforts of the Association did not stop at speeches and calls for action. Individual members went to incredible lengths to solve their own problems. One head mistress in answer to the question "How many applicants did you have for this post?" replied stoutly, "None, I found him!", and this was typical of many. Some members joined with head masters on panels of persuasive speakers who visited schools and universities to reveal the attractions of teaching as a career. Most of all they steadily encouraged their own pupils to enter the profession and answer the national need. In 1960, with the enthusiastic co-operation of Sheila Wood, Secretary of the Association of Assistant Mistresses, a joint committee was formed (Joint Two) with Joyce Bishop (Godolphin and Latymer School), tireless and well acquainted with the corridors of power, as its chairman. They set out to act as a ginger group to the rather languid official efforts to recruit married women and to publicize both the need and the possible remedies. They were particularly interested in women graduates who might return to teaching and in the conditions which would encourage them. With the help of a grant from the Gulbenkian Trust they circulated an inquiry to a significant sample and the response was encouraging. *The Times* published an article by Joyce Bishop in which she neatly disposed of the picture of girls' schools staffed solely by seasoned spinsters and wrote that the married teacher was "welcomed on arrival and wooed to return after rearing her family." The findings of the inquiry and the persistence of the Joint Two undoubtedly spurred on the Ministry to make greater efforts to recruit married women, the local authorities to employ them and provide refresher courses, the schools to fit them in and help them to adjust. One result was a remarkable increase between 1960 and 1968 in the number of part-time and full-time married women in the schools, another was that the attractions of teaching as a career were undoubtedly emphasized when it was seen to be compatible with marriage.

Gradually the challenge of the Butler Act was met, the essentials which made secondary education a reality were achieved. It was costly in money and costly in energy and strength and always the horizons receded. The public demand for education grew, the schools grew and so did their responsibilities and the demands made on them. The questioning of curriculum and the probing into methods intensified; the strains and stresses of society, moral and political, were felt more acutely in the schools. Alice Meynell once wrote:

> I cannot see
> I, child of process—if there lies
> An end for me
> Full of repose, full of replies.

In the second half of the twentieth century head mistresses, involved as always with individuals, with the families and groups from which they spring, and with the total society of which we all are part, were sure they could not see such an end.

Chapter 8

Circular 10/65 and all that

In July 1965 the Secretary of State for Education and Science, Anthony Crosland, issued Circular 10/65 "requiring" local authorities to prepare and submit if they had not already done so "plans for reorganizing secondary education in their areas on comprehensive lines." The Labour Government's objective was made explicit. It was "to end selection at 11 plus and to eliminate separatism in secondary education," and with this a long step forward towards the dissolution of the tripartite system was taken.

This book is not a history of education or of politics but of a hundred years in the life of one teachers' association. Yet all through it has been obvious, and indeed it has been stated, that the evolution of the Association of Head Mistresses must be seen, and can only be understood, "against the background of contemporary events" and so the background of Circular 10/65 must briefly be described.

The tripartite system was never explicitly mentioned in the Education Act of 1944—it was in fact the Norwood Report, published in 1943 and described later as "a clever piece of rationalization," which first set the system out in detail and in exceptionally urbane language—but almost everywhere the provisions of the Act were applied in a tripartite framework. London, Anglesey and the Isle of Man were notably early exceptions, all three for particular reasons. The Act was received with enthusiasm, but almost as soon as it became law the campaign to dismantle the framework in which it operated began to accelerate. Yet this was inevitable. Given the changing structure of society, the spread of egalitarianism, the massive increase of interest in education, the urgent need to realize to the full our national resources and the suspicion that we were wasting much human potential—the tripartite system or, as it was in most areas, the bipartite system of selective and non-selective schools, could not have remained permanently acceptable.

Other factors added momentum to the demand for further change. Between 1944 and 1964 there developed some outstanding secondary modern schools where the education given was of high quality, where genuine advances were made in curriculum and methods of teaching (free at first from the restraints of examinations), where school and community worked in close accord. There were many more which were sound and viable if not specially enterprising or original. But always the modern schools were compared by the public with the grammar schools, established, successful, flourishing, with clear objectives and leading to accepted qualifications, higher education and prestigious jobs. By that comparison modern schools were found wanting by a large majority of parents who persisted in believing they were second best. And indeed in those areas where money was doled out more sparingly to them than to grammar schools (and in 1955 one of the best local authorities was spending an annual average of £4.4s.0d. on books and materials for a pupil in a grammar school against £3.1s.0d. for one in a modern school), where their staffing ratios were unfavourable, or where the percentage admitted to the selective schools was so high that good ability was scarce in the non-selective, this belief was understandable, indeed justified. Parents were not to be fooled, and they were perfectly well aware that grammar schools offered opportunities and often facilities that modern schools did not. They resolutely refused to give "parity of esteem" even when, in answer to public pressure, the modern schools cast away their freedom of curriculum in favour of public examinations.

The attitudes of press, radio and television did not always help, though their efforts were well-meaning. Journalists, for instance, might honestly try to write constructively about the achievements of the modern schools but when their articles were given such titles as "Is your child doomed to a modern school?" or "Don't despise the modern school" the effect was the opposite of what, presumably, they intended. One article began by saying that its aim was "to bring some hope and comfort to these young people [in modern schools] and their parents" but the first hope offered was escape!—by transfer to a selective school. Indeed the prophecy made by the Education Committee of the London County Council in 1943 that in spite of all persuasion "secondary modern schools will be places which all or many will try to avoid," in the main came true.

The frustration of many parents, and many teachers too, built up into strong pressure against the methods of selection by which children were allocated to secondary schools and "the eleven plus" which had first been thought of as a mechanism for justice (fairer by far to select by ability than by wealth and social ambition) came to be seen as a tyranny. As the opposition strengthened, the defence of selective methods weakened until it came to the point when no amount of bluff about "the best interests of the child" and "parity of esteem between schools" could hide the misgivings of teachers, psychologists and administrators. Nor could it conceal their growing conviction not only that an infallible method of selection did not and probably never would exist but that selection itself was wrong. When this became the prevailing view there was only one alternative—to end selection and to adopt a comprehensive system in some form.

After 1944 the Labour party never ceased to voice its dislike of the tripartite system or disguise its intention to abolish it as soon as possible. In 1964 this was part of its election policy. When Labour won the General Election and formed a govern-ment it was clear that the heat was on, in spite of rather unconvincing attempts to gloss over what were thought might be the unpopular effects of reorganization. Thus Harold Wilson's dead body was to be interposed between grammar schools and destruction, and Richard Crossman wrote in *The Times Educational Supplement,* "The Labour party is opposed to any form of reorganization which would level down academic standards."

There may have been some head mistresses in some schools so engrossed in their immediate work or so aloof from current trends that Circular 10/65 found them completely unprepared, but most of them followed the movement of events and were well aware of the way things were shaping. London's example had been followed by Bristol and the West Riding of Yorkshire and other local authorities, and by 1963 there were 175 comprehensive schools in England and Wales. Fifty authorities had at least some and more were considering them, a number which increased after the General election. Two prominent members of the Association, Margaret Miles (Mayfield School, Putney) and Mary Green (Kidbrooke School) had for some years been heads of very large and successful comprehensive schools and ardently supported them. Some of their colleagues felt little sympathy with their enthusiasm, some even felt uneasily that they had sold a pass. Others however were not so sure. Some remembered that before the war there had been support for "the multi-bias school" in the Association, and probably a great many agreed when Mary Price (Milham Ford School, Oxford), speaking in 1954 at the Conference, said in an intentional understatement, "Few people feel perfectly happy about the tripartite system." Nevertheless the general feeling of the Association in 1964 to 1965—and it was not alone in this—was that comprehensive secondary schools were not yet sufficiently proven for them to be adopted wholesale and everywhere. They were seen as too large and therefore too impersonal, for at that time the concept of the size of school necessary to produce a viable sixth form was 1,800 to 2,000. This is now much modified. Not unnaturally, since as a nation we have a deep reverence for anything that has worked for a long—or comparatively long—time, most head mistresses recoiled from the notion that educational communities with known objectives and of proved success would be lost by reorganization.

In October 1964 the Association with their colleagues in Joint Four and the National Union of Teachers issued a statement on "Reorganization of Secondary Education" in which they set out the basic criteria which would in their view make this acceptable. The associations had not forgotten the long period of preparation for the great Act of 1944, the Green Paper, the White Paper, the fruitful discussions, the prolonged and thoughtful debate in Parliament. Now the Government, without a fraction of these preliminaries, was issuing proposals at least as fundamental and far-reaching without so much as a White Paper, and schemes were being devised by some local authorities with a speed so precipitate as to shock many who were in sympathy with their intention. The NUT spoke out sharply against "crack-pot schemes hastily conceived and hastily executed" and the joint statement stressed first of all the importance of proper and unhurried consultations. "Consultations with the teachers through their professional associations should begin at the earliest possible moment ... before there are any moves towards reorganization"! At this distance away from 1964 to 1965 it is perhaps difficult to believe that any local authorities could have been so crass as to draw up plans for education without discussing them with those who had a wealth of experience and expertise to offer, and who in the end would have to make them work. The best authorities, of course, did nothing of the kind, but from the first drew upon the knowledge and advice of their teachers and arrived at decisions after full and informed discussion. Yet in some places schemes were, and still are, announced either without any consultation at all, or after discussions which were so perfunctory or within such circumscribed limits as to be derisory. Such authorities fail entirely to grasp the simple truth set down in Stewart Mason's preface in the booklet on the Leicestershire plan, "It is only possible to introduce such basic change if you can carry with you a preponderance of goodwill both from the teaching profession and the public." "There is a vast difference," said Jennett Evans (Keighley Girls' Grammar School) in 1964, "between an imposed decision and a decision arrived at after fully informed and sympathetic discussion." Her own school, which had been founded in 1871, had just been reorganized into a mixed comprehensive school by an authority which had followed the second method. There were times too when, even though discussion was full and frank, the confusion and bias in the minds of some members of education committees could shake even the most cynical. "I do not suppose," said one councillor to a head mistress, "that education in the city will be nearly as good after reorganization as it is now, but at least it will be fair," and the same unquestioning passion for egalitarianism was behind a proposal made in 1972 that the

The Evolution of a School
(*By permission of the Governors of Mayfield School, Putney*)

staffs of grammar schools should be cut in the interim period before they took an unselective entry so as "not to give them an unfair start"!

Another anxiety in the Association was the question of finance, for it was obvious that to implement reorganization fully would be very expensive and that the temptation to penurious authorities to make do with as little expenditure as possible on buildings and equipment would simply add to the "cock-eyed" schemes. In May 1965 a Joint Four delegation met the Secretary of State to raise with him certain points of crucial importance, among them the now hoary matters of consultation, the scrutiny of unsuitable schemes, the danger of neighbourhood schools with catchment areas badly drawn, and the urgent question of money.

In answer to a direct question, "Will financial provision be increased to meet the expense of what must be, if properly carried out, a very costly undertaking?", the Minister's reply left no doubt that it would not be increased, and the Joint Four left Whitehall uncomforted and quite clear that the familiar shortage of money would dog the schools in the great changes which again confronted them. They had less heart for the struggle than in 1944.

It was, in fact, impossible not to have continuing reservations, not so much about the principle of comprehensive education as about the methods which were used to achieve it. The stream of anxious letters asking for advice which reached the Association's office in Gordon Square did not come from inadequate or uncompromising head mistresses but from women who were deeply concerned for education in their areas. They not only reflected personal anxiety, as they well might have done, for some head mistresses found themselves suddenly insecure with the future in jeopardy, and some had the unnerving experience of reading in the newspaper, before receiving any direct information from their employing authority, that their schools were to disappear and that they had been appointed to other posts for which they had not even applied. It was not only that years of service, of experience, of professional skill appeared to be quite devalued or that, in some circles at least, the implication seemed to be that what they had been doing in the schools was not only outmoded but positively harmful; it was the knowledge that so much constructive work seemed to be undone, so many schools of proved worth or of promise, grammar, modern and technical, were being dismembered with indecent haste and apparently without a thought of their quality.

It was difficult to pretend—it still is—that an educating community divided into two units twelve miles apart and called "a school" really was one in any proper sense, or to acquiesce in a situation, which would be comic if it were not true, where a weekly total of ninety-two hours is spent by the teaching staff in travelling between two sections of a school housed in different buildings at opposite ends of a country town.

The Association has protested vigorously, alone and in company with the other teachers' organizations, against bad schemes, precipitate action and injustice to individuals; but it must not be seen simply as a "party of protest" or as reluctant to the point of resisting change. Reserve is not the same as rejection; and the Association, with 150 or more of its members in charge of comprehensive schools (though not all initially by choice), has accepted with increasing speed that these are the means by which the democratization of education will proceed. Many head mistresses, at first at odds with bureaucrats and planners, have come to terms with their proposals, often managing to modify them in the process. Many work in areas where opinion is unanimous—and has been for a long time—that comprehensive schools best suit the local needs, and many feel that advantages outweigh obvious defects in organization. Some have been converted from doubt, dislike and cautious reserve to genuine enthusiasm. They have shaken free of any lingering idea that the comprehensive school is simply a much enlarged grammar school to be run on the same lines and recognize it as a quite different sort of educating community requiring very different organization and very varied expertise. When they list the advantages, they put high the liberating effect on girls and boys not selected for grammar schools when they escape a sense of failure; the unifying effect on heads and staff freed from the divisiveness of working in different kinds of schools, "some thought superior and others inferior"; the striking results in both pupils and teachers of greatly increased resources and opportunities. Nearly all these

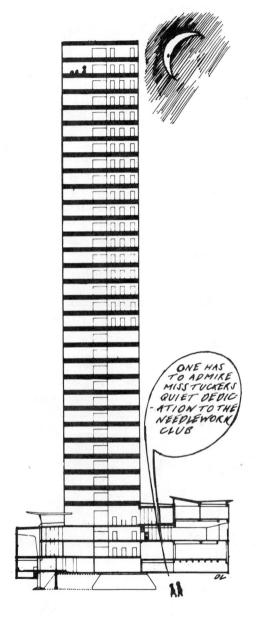

The individual is not lost.
(*Drawing by David Lamb*)

head mistresses work in areas where the local authority has planned and implemented reorganization with understanding, sympathy, and consultation with teachers, where they have not as soon as a comprehensive school was named and launched appeared to wash their hands of the project as if it was then complete. Such authorities have continued to play their part in supporting head and staff through initial difficulties and frustrations until the school was established as a thriving community.

Yet there still remain questions to be asked about what Shirley Williams, MP for Hitchen, has called "the compulsive alterations in institutions" and they demand answers. The process of reorganization of secondary education has certainly been compulsive, protracted, and even now is incomplete. In some areas plan after plan has been proposed and come to nothing, so that disillusioned teachers live in an atmosphere of continual uncertainty. It is not surprising to hear that one head mistress, who called her staff together to tell them of the latest proposal for their area, found them divided into optimists, pessimists, and those cynics who said, "This is the seventh plan in ten years and no more likely than the others to be put into practice"!

A confused situation and almost uncountable variations in organization were made worse rather than better by the withdrawal of Circular 10/65 and by the piecemeal acceptance or rejection of the proposals of local authorities by the Secretary of State, decisions which often seem inconsistent with overall plans and indeed make havoc of them. Will the losses which result from delay, uncertainty and upheaval—and there are inescapable losses—in the end be made good for the pupils in the schools? Will opportunities, everywhere so vastly increased for girls and boys in the middle and lower ranges of ability, be everywhere as great for those of high ability? The existence of independent and direct grant schools has always made it necessary for maintained schools to compete with them in the field of higher education and careers. Will the dice be loaded even more in favour of the pupils in these schools with their selected entry and consequently narrower objectives? And how can comprehensive schools succeed—or indeed be said to exist at all—in those areas where selective schools are retained and a balanced intake made impossible?

"Equality of opportunity" is almost a dying catchword; perhaps it should be replaced by "Opportunity for equality," and, if it is, can neighbourhood schools in under-privileged or one-class areas give their pupils that opportunity? Young people, if they are to feel themselves members of a community, with all that it implies of happiness and responsibility, must be in that community long enough to feel secure and accepted. How short a time is "long enough"? Two years, as in some places?

Comprehensive education is now going on in a wide range of different patterns, interesting in their diversity, no doubt, but seriously complicating for children in a society which is increasingly mobile. Is it not time to pause and assess the advantages and disadvantages of these different forms of comprehensive institutions, not with the view of imposing uniformity but simply to pick out those that seem to work best and learn from them?

In his book *Other Schools and Ours*, comparing education in seven countries, Edmund King wrote that there was "nowhere where such colossal changes of pattern and methods in education," both necessary for the modern world, went on as quietly as in Britain, nowhere where they engendered so little bitterness and conflict. This may well be true, yet the reorganization of education in the past twenty years has caused both bitterness and conflict. Some of the conflict has had less to do with the education of children than with politics at both local and central levels which seems now as never before to affect what happens *to* schools and even *in* them.

An American critic of English universities in the 1930s wrote, "The English believe in religion, in manners, and in politics; throughout their history education has been subordinated now to one, now to another of the three." Subordination to either of the first two has surely disappeared but subordination to the third seems over-powerful. Are the constant manoeuvrings and uncertainties which it produces to be permanent features of education in the future?

These are some of the questions which the Association is asking in 1974, not in a spirit of reaction but because of its continuing concern for quality, for freedom, for the individual. It is a concern which needs to be asserted as strenuously now as at any time in the first hundred years of its existence.

Chapter 9

Not in isolation

The first thing to do is to form the committees:
The consultative councils, the standing committees, select committees and sub-committees.

Coriolan: Difficulties of a Statesman, by T.S. Eliot

If committees are a mark of progress, head mistresses cannot be accused of hanging back. In 1944 and after, while they were engaged in countless tasks within their schools, they also had to reach out and deal with other matters which would not wait. Almost before they were aware of it they were caught up in the new attitude towards education, the growing interest of the public, the determination of parents to be told what was going on, the rising clamour for "participation."

In this, head mistresses almost without exception were involved at local level, discussing plans with local authorities, holding parents' meetings, and working on a multiplicity of committees. Many heads held influential local positions; they might be members of Education Committees or of Hospital Boards; they might be Justices of the Peace, with particular interest in Juvenile Courts, or connected with some branch of social service which was just as much engaged in readjustment after the war as were the educationists. These were individual responsibilities but they all made demands on time and energy.

With regard to the claims of the Association, considerable activity went on in the regional branches, where members were able to pool their experiences and offer each other advice and assistance in the many adjustments that had to be made. The Branches are a distinctive feature in the organization of the Association, developing as the numbers grew, according to the needs and circumstances of the different localities. They came into being from about 1910 onwards; in 1917 and 1918 they were recognized as "electoral areas," and their presidents were elected members of Executive. The two earliest, both formed in 1913, were London and a combination of the counties of Lancashire, Cheshire and Derbyshire.

There are now thirteen branches, including Wales and Scotland, each with its own character. Membership of branches is on a wider basis than that of the Association as a whole, for they have for many years been free to elect, as an affiliated member of the branch, the head mistress of any kind of educational institution giving secondary education but not coming within the terms of Ordinary membership, the chief assistant mistress of a mixed secondary school under the headship of a man, and any other person whose election may have received previous sanction from the Executive Committee of the Association. Thus schools of different types have been brought together and co-operation has been fostered in the locality. So valuable have these wider contacts proved in the branches that in 1971 the Association instituted a category of Affiliates to the central organization and by 1972 there were sixty-two such Affiliates, for the most part the senior mistresses and deputy heads of large maintained co-educational schools under the headship of a man; they now include one or two examples of a recent phenomenon, the head master of a girls' boarding school. It is in the branches that some head mistresses have had their greatest influence, preferring the personal contacts and friend-liness of a smaller sphere to work at Executive level, and the experience and prestige of a head who has won the confidence of the area over many years are of the utmost value to the Association as a whole as well as to her colleagues.

But, inevitably, wider contacts have to be made and maintained, and some heads get their first taste of central administration by being elected to the central Executive as representatives of their branch. A survey of a typical agenda for an Executive Committee meeting, actually one held in 1971, illustrates what then lies before them.

Over and above the normal routine business of such a meeting—finance, membership, reports from representatives on other bodies—there were familiar items appearing very differently in modern contexts: public examinations, university entrance, discipline, the School Health Service, careers and the persistent prejudice in some fields against girls and women. These were followed by problems of to-day: the effects of pornographic literature and of some magazines for young people (half a century ago the question had been of the educational and moral effects of cinematograph performances on which evidence had been given to a Commission of Inquiry), the cause and cure of drug addiction, a request for oral evidence to be given to a Working Party on the Unplanned Pregnancy, the James Inquiry (later Report) on Teacher Training, the admission of women to men's colleges at Cambridge, and, for good measure, Metrication (in 1907 the Executive had given its blessing to Decimalization). Comment had been sought on the White Paper on the Reorganization of Local Government, and evidence requested for a working party of the Department of the Environment, on "The Role of Voluntary Movements and Youth." The possible shape of things to come is indicated by the inclusion on a very crowded agenda of a talk on "A Ministry of Education for Europe," and by the presence at Executive for the first time of observers from the Head Masters' Association. Over sixty members of Executive were present.

This is a great contrast to 14 May 1887, when there were only fifteen present. There is a contrast, too, in the agenda. Here is a summary of the Proceedings, still written by hand at that stage:

Miss Buss (President) and fourteen others were present.

1. Membership of Executive. According to the constitution of the Association framed the previous year, four members of Executive must retire and four others be elected in their place at the next Conference. How to decide which four should retire? Resolved that it should be the four who had attended the least number of committees during the year.

[The defaulters are then named and arrangements made for the election of their successors.]
2. Copies of two pamphlets, "Occupation for Women" and "The Balance of Activity" to be sent to each member of the Association.
3. The loyal address to the Queen on her Jubilee. Miss Porter's draft approved and the expenditure of not more than five guineas to have it engrossed.
4. Reports had been prepared on Home Time Tables, Elementary School Scholars and Charitable Work in schools. These were to be read at the Uppingham Conference. The programme and agenda for the Conference were approved, including the report from Executive.

The key to this changed situation is that a head mistress of the 1970s is a woman of her time, committed in the first place to the interests of her school, but linking this with a wide range of service and activities, local, national or international; in short, a woman who expects to be concerned with public as well as scholastic affairs. She may be a married woman, sharing with her husband the responsibilities of a home and family; she may be caring for dependants. In one way or another, she leads her own life in addition to her career. Another reason for the change is the ever-growing sense that the school is a part of the community and its head a citizen with special, but widely ranging, responsibilities; that education is in fact an inseparable part of the process of civilized life. The ready outcry, "Why don't the schools do something about it?" has so far become fact that head mistresses are forced to include in their orbit anything that pertains to their pupils in or out of school, in this country or abroad, and anything that concerns teachers as a professional body. This means that the Association cannot escape being involved with the whole range of education from nursery to university. It includes a secondary school field increasingly specialized in such techniques as methods of assessment, educational technology, management, career guidance, counselling. It includes contacts with other services concerned with young people, such as the law, the church, medicine, youth clubs, voluntary service here and overseas. Its members serve on University Courts, Examination Boards, the governing bodies of Colleges of Education and other educational institutes. The range of interests is wide, and all members of the Association involved to a greater or less degree, for each is a cell of activity touching the life of the community in a multiplicity of ways. Obviously attention can be directed only to one or two main spheres of interest and influence.

In quite early days good working relationships were established at local level with the Ministry of Labour, through the Head Mistresses' Employment Committees, set up from 1918 in various areas and owing much to the initiative of Ethel Strudwick (City of London and St Paul's Schools). She was not only a distinguished scholar, but also a woman of "strong and experienced judgement," a "liberal" in the fullest sense of the word in her concerns and her character. Ethel Jones (Clapham County School) who worked with her on these committees said, "Always one found the quick grasp of essentials and the human understanding and sympathy which never allowed the welfare of the individual to be lost sight of in a wealth of red tape."

Consultations also took place with hospital matrons, again through local committees in the first place, and when these and the employment committees later developed into large national organizations the friendliness and understanding at first engendered remained. Amy Bull (Wallington County School) and Eileen Harold (Haberdashers' Aske's School, Acton) have achieved a great deal in this field, and the former since her retirement has devoted much of her time to hospital management and nursing interests. This is in keeping with her wide sympathies demonstrated also by her creation of the Amy Bull Fund for retired head mistresses, her work on the Public Services Pensioners Council, and her long service on the Surrey Education Committee.

Highly important are the links with the other professional associations, particularly the other occupants of Gordon House, the Head Masters' Association, the Association of Assistant Mistresses and the Association of Assistant Masters. As early as 1904 there was a joint conference of the Associations of Head Mistresses and of Head Masters with the National Union of Elementary Teachers, the College of Preceptors, and the Teachers' Guild—a body including both men and women working for the unity of the teaching profession. By 1917 there existed a Federal Council of Secondary Schools Associations, which included the Association of Head Mistresses among its constituent bodies. In the Proceedings of Executive for May 1917 there is a reference to a "Joint Conference of Representatives of the Four Secondary School Associations," called to consider co-operation in ·matters of common interest. It was decided to ask the various Executives to appoint representatives on a permanent joint committee which should have power to take action in matters of urgency. This is the emergence of the Joint Four, and although the mention of this name to anyone outside the profession may produce no reaction except a blank stare, it is in fact a powerful force in secondary education, both nationally and internationally. It is a Central Joint Committee of the four secondary associations; a head master alternates with a head mistress as chairman, and the two honorary secretaries are appointed from the assistants' associations. At times, no doubt, one or other of the four associations would find it easier to act alone, but this desire is generally curbed by the overriding importance of speaking as a united group of secondary school teachers on the great questions of the day.

The Joint Four has had a voice on the Burnham Committee since its inception in 1919 and now sends four representatives, one of whom is a head mistress. In 1920 Grace Fanner was able to report that the Teachers' Panel of the Burnham Committee was unanimously in favour of equal pay for equal work—a conclusion which would have given pleasure to those early heads who fought so doughtily for the principle—though in practice it was not to be fully implemented for another forty-one years. The first Burnham Representative of the Association was Beatrice Sparks (Cheltenham Ladies' College) who had no easy task in helping to set up that Burnham Committee, and the role of the Burnham representative is always an exacting one.

Several distinguished head mistresses have chosen to devote themselves to the work of Joint Four, including the office of chairman, because they have seen in it an unrivalled opportunity of co-operation between professional associations, and therefore of powerful influence. Since 1919 there have been local Joint Fours, which play an important part in the affairs of their area. The close relationship with the other members of Joint Four built up both locally and centrally has been continuous and fruitful. There have also been valuable, though less close and continuous, connections and consultations with other teachers' associations.

Increasingly links have been forged with all institutions of higher education, one of the strongest being the annual conferences, held for many years, with the principals and tutors of the women's colleges of Oxford, Cambridge and London, and now further extended. Over the years, individual vice-chancellors have been good friends to the schools, some of them to girls' education in particular, and there is now a Joint Standing Committee of Vice-Chancellors with head masters and head mistresses, marking the latest stage in the history of direct co-operation between schools and universities. In these and other ways, channels of communication are kept open, and different stages in the world of education recognize more and more their dependence on each other. There are, for instance, the meeting-points provided through the Council for National Academic Awards, on which Beryl Williams has served in her own right; the Universities Central Council for Admissions, the Association of Training Colleges and Departments of Education, and the Council for Educational Advance, all growing in importance.

A body of national scope on which the Association had representation from the beginning was the Secondary Schools Examination Council, formed in 1917. It was reconstituted in 1964 as the Schools Council on which the first representative was Mary Price, the second Diana Reader Harris (Sherborne School for Girls). The terms of reference now extend beyond examinations to the much broader matter of the curriculum, and this has led to a great proliferation of committees, in which an increasing number of head mistresses and assistants have been involved. The weight of paper issued by the Council has become a byword amongst those who have not only to read it but also to attend meetings staggering under the load they carry.

There remain Educational Commissions, going back to 1894, with the trembling Frances Mary Buss giving evidence to the Taunton Commission, and as these have multiplied, so the influence of the Association has increased. It has been invited to submit evidence, both oral and written, for all these inves-tigations, and the written evidence has been widely circulated to members and to other interested persons. At times it has even been a "best-seller."

In addition to this, individuals have played their part not

only in giving evidence, but serving as members of a commission, sometimes as representatives, but more often in their own right. Such work, though heavy, is exhilarating, and few would now echo the words of Sara Burstall, "I left my youth in the Conference room of the Board of Education."

Dorothy Brock was a member of the Consultative Committee which produced the Spens Report (1938). Mary Clarke served on the Norwood Committee (1943). Dorothy Brock and Emmeline Tanner on the Fleming Committee (1946). The setting-up of the Central Advisory Council gave rise to a spate of reports, some better known than others. Agnes Bozman (Manchester High School) was a member of the committee responsible for the report entitled *Early Leaving* (1954). Mary Green and Emily Huxstep (Chislehurst County School) were members of the Crowther Committee (1959), and Mary Green also of the Newsom (1963). The latest report was the Donnison (1970), the second report of the Public Schools Commission, and Jean Wilks (King Edward's, Birmingham) was a member of that committee.

No list of this kind would be complete without some mention of Kitty Anderson (North London Collegiate School), who has taken a prominent part in much educational work. She was a member of the Robbins Committee (1963), the first woman to serve on the University Grants Committee, followed by Joyce Bishop and then Joyce Bradbury (Thornhill School, Sunderland), and a member of the Public Schools Commission (1969). She combines with these and other distinctions a continuing interest in historical research, and, true to her Yorkshire heritage, great skill in the domestic arts. It is said that she arrived one December day at a committee meeting held at the Department of Education and Science bearing a basket of home-made mince-pies which she distributed to her fellow members.

From the national to the international was a natural, indeed an inevitable, step. Contacts of various sorts had been made by individuals from quite early days, and in 1897 an official connection was formed between the Association and India; in 1907 the India and Overseas Committee was set up, eventually to become the International Committee, a regular committee of Executive. It was, however, the experience of two world wars that widened horizons and intensified the need for under-standing. After 1918 many head mistresses were inspired by the belief that the cause of world peace could be advanced by a right education of the younger generation, and dedicated themselves to this work. Mention has already been made of the outstanding part played by Lilian Charlesworth in the Council for Education in World Citizenship. In 1931 there took place an official tour of Canada in which twelve head mistresses joined. A number have taken a share in the work of the British Council, travelling far and wide for conferences, lectures and visitations.

Most significant perhaps, because most continuous, among the Association's international activities has been its vigorous share in the two great organizations of the International Federation of Secondary School Teachers (better known under its French initials FIPESO) and the World Confederation of Organizations of the Teaching Profession (or WCOTP). Since 1934 the Association, acting as one element of Joint Four, has been regularly involved in the work of FIPESO with its mutual study of educational theory and practice in the member countries, its stimulating conferences held in almost every country of Europe, and the active friendship and sense of unity these engender. Margaret Adams was instrumental in the revival of FIPESO after the Second World War and was its President from 1952 to 1956. Harold Elvin, in one of his travel books, records a remark made by a Russian, "As they say in the parts I come from, friendship between nations begins with a single handshake." It is this friendly handshake which Margaret Adams has offered so willingly, and no member of the Association has done more to foster understanding between teachers all over the world.

It was in 1952 that the World Organization finally took shape. FIPESO is predominantly European; WCOTP embraces also the American and Afro-Asian countries. All these activities are part of the steadily growing current of thought and action which has carried the Association and its members into the wider reaches of international life. The spirit which has inspired this movement is not different from that of the early pioneers; it is rather its logical extension.

It is difficult to assess the influence exercised by the Association. One can pick up books on educational history and not find it even mentioned. Everyone knows what the letters NUT stand for; few outside the profession recognize AHM. This is partly because it is a small association; the sheer numbers of some organizations give them prominence, but the AHM only has about 850 members in active service, including those overseas. It seldom hits the headlines, perhaps because it is concerned principally with matters which lie at the heart of education—and true education still is not "news." Often it has been unpopular and in advance of its time, advocating measures for which the majority were not ready, but which were eventually adopted and are now common practice—no one remembers where they originated.

An unusual factor in its influence is the extent to which it has depended on individuals or small groups, as well as on the Association as a whole. Because of its small size, it often has only one representative where larger bodies have several, so that its success in a particular field may vary considerably according to the representative of the moment. There is also the indirect influence, exercised by individuals who hold a high position in some spheres which they have made their special concern, and which is basically educational. Such, for example, has been the work done by Rachel Pearse (Mary Datchelor School) on the Home Office Committee of the Probation Service, by Diana Reader Harris as President of the Church Missionary Society and by Margaret Miles as Chairman of the Nuffield Resources for Learning Committee.

Of particular importance is the field of broadcasting and television, with its ever-growing hold on public attention and thoughts. Here the Association has been well served, for Mary Green is a Governor of the British Broadcasting Council, Margaret Miles sits on the Education Committee of the Independent Television Authority and other head mistresses have taken their turn on the Schools Broadcasting Council of the United Kingdom since its inception. Of these, Rachel Pearse served for six years and was chairman of the Secondary Education Programme Committee. There is little doubt that by one means or another, the opinions and counsels of the Association have permeated educational thinking and affected national policy.

The annual Conference provides an obvious occasion for

renewing and augmenting contacts. A welcome is given to representatives of many organizations who, over the years, have become friends and who are invited to the Conference, as well as to speakers who come to address the gathering. It also gives members the opportunity to meet the Secretary of the Association and her assistants, who transport themselves, bag and baggage, to the Conference centre, and there set up a temporary office. Hitherto, members may only have been aware of these key people as signatures on letters or voices on the telephone, but now they meet them personally, and catch a glimpse of what is always going on behind the scenes, the personal concern for the anxieties of individuals, the patience, good humour and knowledge which are never-failing. Out of the hundred years of Association history, seventy-two have been covered by three secretaries, Louisa Brough for twenty-seven years, Ruth Young for thirty-one and Jean McF. Miller for fourteen. The present secretary is Lucile Spalding, who has been in office since 1961.

The atmosphere of the Conference is not a formal one and there is little of the protocol and set procedure which are the mark of those massive confabulations held regularly in conference centres. The amenities of such centres have sometimes been lacking, but until recent years the Association has sacrificed these in order to continue the early tradition of meeting, whenever possible, in a school, and of visiting different localities, choosing London in alternate years. In early days the chosen town in the provinces sometimes had little suitable hotel accommodation, and members relied on the hospitality generously offered by parents and friends of the hostess school. The one essential was a good hall, big enough to house the conference, but in many instances the school could not provide a large dining-room as well, and the catering arrangements called for resource and ingenuity. None of this was apparent on the surface; the impression taken away by members was of a warm welcome, boundless hospitality and smiling stewards. Universities and colleges have often issued invitations to the Conference, which could not always be accepted because of awkward dates, but when these have been possible the conference has been very successful. It now meets in alternate years in the Queen Elizabeth Hall, London. In the intervening years it still moves about the country, capturing the flavour of different centres—Edinburgh, Bristol, Cardiff, Scarborough, Manchester, Norwich. The Conference service, now oecumenical in its nature, has an important place in the proceedings.

As well as hearing speeches from distinguished visitors the Association has never lacked its own good speakers, forceful, witty and wise. Sometimes a whole speech has been memorable; sometimes it is just a phrase that remains lodged in the memory, to recur later in the hour of need; for example, Mary Hanbridge (Central Foundation School, London) giving advice to young heads, "Don't be afraid to take the bull by the horns. You will often find it is nothing but a little bleating calf"; or Ethel Strudwick, in her deep resonant voice, "Remember that interruptions will be the greater part of your work"; the same thought differently expressed by Frances Hiley (Central Newcastle High School), who commended "the costly grace of accessibility" as one of the virtues of a head mistress.

Although the two days of the Conference are strenuous they are also stimulating and members return with new ideas to their separate schools. There the pattern of life awaiting them leaves little time for contemplation. The following extracts, taken at random from the diaries of the head mistresses of three different kinds of schools, give a glimpse of the world in which every member of the Association finds her greatest scope, the cell from which her influence spreads.

From the diary of the head of a girls' grammar school in the North. One day in February.

Blizzard. Children arrive late and smiling from the Pennines with news that they have got here but think the road will be closed in an hour or two.

Endless consultations with bus company as to which buses are getting through and whether children should be sent home or wait. Endless queues of children clamouring to leave early. Problem—let them go and get cold waiting for buses still travelling to normal schedule, or keep them and risk their being without transport. Decide on second course. Wrong decision according to indignant parent.

Invasion by sheep on way to market. Flock enter front hall where they are most unwelcome.

Parent rings up in some distress to request leave of absence for his daughter as they are selling the farm and he would like all the family together on the day the stock is disposed of.

Parent of boarder who ran away to London, but is now back in boarding house, will not communicate with me, nor her, nor send any money. Welfare departments pass the buck to one another blandly. I worry about the holidays.

Follow-up from County Hall about a boarder's parent who had not paid fees. Solicitor's letter produced a visit to County Hall and £75 of the £80 owing. (He sold some cattle last market-day.)

Day ends with a fire. Waste paper, thrown down shute into boiler room, in flames though boiler not lighted. Fire engine arrives, too late but very impressive and exciting, especially for unsuspecting official from County Hall who follows it to front door.

(School routine continues unperturbed by these incidents, though I am a little *distraite* in some of my lessons.)

A Mixed Comprehensive School in the Midlands One day in September

8.15 a.m.   Interview with teacher of Social Adjustment Unit. This is new this term, will have a maximum of ten and at present only has five children. I spent half-an-hour chatting with children yesterday, and felt real progress was being made in getting them to make a relationship with each other—but later D. went berserk and attacked another child. Head of House will have him this morning till things have calmed down.

9.30 a.m.   Fire Drill after House Assemblies. First one planned by new Senior (formerly Head of House). Very well planned, children good, lovely day. Find one Deputy, Senior Master and myself all converging on an old boy who has infiltrated the lines. I think Christopher rather enjoys the furore; he had been passing and had joined in for old times sake! Who says we don't know the pupils in a large school?

10.30 a.m.   Post—Amongst this, query from LEA. Will I have two visitors from HMA Working Party on Disadvantage? I'm pleased to hear my colleagues are investigating this problem, and will be glad to see them. Am reminded that local inspector is coming in about 11.15.

11.15 a.m.   Local inspector has come, as I guessed, to break news about reorganization plan before the Press has it this afternoon. The secret's been extraordinarily well kept, largely because working party has been meeting throughout holidays. The suggested plan will make for an awkward amalgamation and puts all our jobs in jeopardy.

12.30 a.m.   Principal of adult education institute for area rings me up. I shall probably have to chair Finance Sub-Committee of Community Centre this evening he says, as the councillor is busy with reorganization meetings.

1.45 p.m. Gather together staff to tell them plan before they see it in the papers. We can discuss it at greater length tomorrow in full Staff Meeting.

2.30 p.m. Appointment with Richard's new probation officer. On this first visit Head of House and I see him together; afterwards he will keep up contact with Head of House. He shows me psychologist's report on Richard. Am mildly surprised to hear that he has "no delinquent trends," considering that he has just been up before the court for burglary, was seen and identified last term by caretaker carrying away our amplifier at 9.30 p.m., but dropped it and ran away, and was transferred to us from a school which he never attended. Recommend to Probation Officer that he needs the regular framework of a hostel, from which he could still come to school. He probably won't get into one.

3.20 p.m. Head of English comes to explain his schemes for this term. He has teams working all through the school, led by different members of his department, and he really brings the best out of them all, and is most generous in his praise of their qualities. He certainly has a marvellous gift for this; all the students get A grades for their teaching practice, and his probationers get a very good report.

4.00 p.m. Normal after-school quiet cup of tea with Deputies and Senior Master chatting and talking over the day, is interrupted by steady flow of staff, some of whom have tea, and some don't, to talk about amalgamation and consortia. They all need keeping on an even keel.

5.30 p.m. Move over to Finance Sub-Committee in Community Centre, which I chair.
Discover that Secondary Education gave Further Education over £1,100 last year as rent for our use of Community Centre! Meeting finishes at 7.30.
I go home.

From the diary of a President of the Association. Two days in late June.

In school by 8.15 a.m., "being accessible." Steady stream of staff and girls, some to make future appointments, some just to bring items of news, e.g. Sponsored walk organized by third year girls raised £70 for hospital in India. Miss X. reports arrangements for holiday exchanges to France at last completed and all problems solved. Mr Y. to say that their baby was born last night; wife and daughter doing well. Prayers taken by VIth Form. Thoughtful and well-prepared; a good start to the day.
9.20. Session with Secretary. Post included questionnaire from Association which I must have approved, but now cannot think why. Also letter of

acceptance (at last) from chief speaker invited for next year's Conference; great comfort to have this settled. Notice of local meeting of NAHT which I must attend as agenda includes reorganization and there will be heated exchanges. Handed over for typing draft of my paper on "Discrimination against Women and Girls in Training for the Medical Profession," finished last night.

10.0. Tried to speak to domestic bursar on school inter-com. system, but wires crossed and got entangled in several peculiar conversations, including one of the staff in deep discussion with her fiancé about their wedding date, and Head of Science Department's trunk call for Birmingham about non-delivery of ordered equipment. Impressed by her command of language. Gave it up and telephoned to Miss B., Chairman of Central Joint Four, to discuss some matters on agenda for next meeting; particularly reorganization of the Health Service and its effect on schools; financial problems of young teachers in their first weeks of teaching; the shape of the School Year and comments on Sir Keith Joseph's talk on "The Cycle of Deprivation."

11.40. Joined staff for break. One of them retails remark of one eleven-year-old to another overheard in corridor outside my room, "Is Miss G. vacant?"

11.40. Session with Deputy Head. I had to leave after lunch for London and she assured me she could cope with anything that might arise—normal or abnormal. Fully agreed with her.

During lunch hour went to the Bank to make arrangements for currency and travellers' cheques for FIPESO trip to Helsinki. *Afternoon.* Train to London: welcome interlude for contemplation. Session at Gordon Square with Secretary. Asked how her research was progressing for her book on Bulstrode Whitelock, the Improbable Puritan, and assisted in translation of some seventeenth-century Latin.

Went through draft agenda for Principals and Tutors Conference in September: also arrangements for informal dinner with representatives of AAM in October. Copies had come of new booklet "A Level Home Economics" from Association of Teachers of Domestic Science, and of "Sports for All" from Sports Council.

Accepted invitation to HMC Confernce, and to HMA meeting and luncheon. Drafted various letters, including one to M.M. asking her to talk to Executive when she returns from the International Commission to advise the Fiji Government on education in the islands.

7.0. Went as guest to dinner of British Medical Association and replied to toast. Pleasant and entertaining evening. I think I drove home a few hard facts.

Next morning Joined by Chairman of Executive of the Association and Miss Z. Went on deputation to Department of Education and Science about difficulties in employing immigrant teachers, and to press for greatly increased opportunities for training courses for them. Given a sympathetic hearing and useful discussion followed; a welcome change from the impasse of reorganization problems.

Caught 2.20 train. Went into school to tidy up odds and ends. Greeted by senior janitor with news that the drainage system in the Biology labs had got schizophrenia (not his exact word) and had discharged half its overflow across the laboratory floors and half into the storeroom. He explained with quiet pride how he had discovered the source of the trouble and put all to rights. Nothing for me to worry about.

Saw the Deputy Head who had been able to cope easily with everything except appeal from domestic bursar to settle dispute between the two janitors over who should shift the dustbins. This had defeated them both. Fear irreparable breakdown of relationships is imminent.

Sign letters and depart for home.

Chapter 10

"We cannot restore old policies or follow an antique drum." [1]

The title chosen for this book may well have caused surprise, hilarity or plain disbelief, according to the cast of mind, among those who think that the word "Revolutionaries" is the last that can or should be applied to head mistresses and who see them as people without marked revolutionary tendencies. Yet there are always radical processes occurring in society without violent upheavals or dramatic publicity which are nevertheless revolutions. It is in some of these that head mistresses, through the past hundred years, have been leaders or catalysts.

The founders of the Association built up their schools and provided education for girls of the middle and upper class against a formidable wall of Victorian prejudice. It was prejudice about the role of women in society, about the dangerous effect that education might have on their willing acceptance of it, and about their essential inadequacy for any intellectual pursuit beyond the study of Mrs Beaton and the use of ready-reckoners for their accounts. A letter published in a women's magazine just two years before the meeting at Myra Lodge put the matter in a nutshell. "We were asked," it ran, "why we disapproved of public schools for girls and not for boys. Our reply was that girls are destined for private and domestic life and boys for public life and that their education should respectively correspond to the duties each has to perform in the future."

[1] *Little Gidding,* by T.S. Eliot.

Since those early days head mistresses, like all other educators, have found themselves launched on a revolutionary course whether they liked it or not, the end of which is nowhere in sight. This is because changes in society have been fundamental and often sudden, education is one of the instruments of change, and therefore the schools are peculiarly susceptible to the results of it. Ever since 1870, as one appetite for education has been largely, if not wholly, satisfied, another has developed, so that 1870 has been followed by 1902 and 1944 as naturally as the day follows the night.

Head mistresses, having battled for education for girls, albeit in a limited section of society, were inevitably caught up in the next step forward, the Act of 1902, which the historian Elie Halévy believed to be "a social revolution of the first magnitude," by which the state first began to make provision for secondary schools. Rejecting the shelter of exclusiveness, they became engaged in the wider field and the more formidable task of making the girls' schools, new and old, maintained and independent, some of the best in the world.

Again, in 1944, they rejected an élitist conception of education, as they then saw élitism, and accepted with enthusiasm and plain words the challenge of the Butler Act. "We stand for secondary education for all up to the age of sixteen; we want that education to be of different types, every one of which shall be accessible to all for whom it is suitable; we ask that the standards of the new secondary schools shall be the best of the old and that they should grow naturally out of a well-planned system of nursery and junior schools; we look forward to the time when the independent and public schools will be associated with the state system, working side by side with it in providing the education for all the children of the nation."

At every stage there have been inescapable tensions. The revolutionary undertaking by nineteenth-century head mistresses to oppose prejudice, to extend those first opportunities to girls, to prove their capacities and to demonstrate that these could be used in a wider field than the family alone, did not make for an easy life. They might be inflexible in their determination but they were not always exhilarated, nor were they militants through and through. Among the faces in the group at the Uppingham conference there are some iron countenances gazing out as if embattled but there are more which are highly intelligent, sensitive and gentle. To these women the cost of stepping out of their quiet family circles into public life must often have been high. Many must sometimes have been as reluctant to face criticism and problems as they were to offend in matters of conventional taste, whether concerned with bicycles or with deportment. "PLS DNT + LGS" ran the cryptic note passed by Dorothea Beale to one of her staff during a lecture at Cheltenham and the response was immediate, "I sat up and uncrossed the offending limbs."

After 1902 there came, as has been shown, tensions of a different kind, professional rather than social, the fear of sacrificing quality in their schools, the fear of losing the freedom and responsibility to which they were accustomed, all the perplexities and often the distresses of working under the retraints of central and local regulations, the detestation of illiberal administration. All of these in some degree and in some places persist.

Since 1944 the pace of change in society and in the schools has greatly accelerated. The centenary of the Association comes at a time when it is not easy to be an educator, and the list of reasons why would be a long one. Problems and uncertainties face all who are responsible in any way for the nurture and development of the young and some of these press upon head mistresses more directly than others, even to the extent of raising the question of their future and the future of their Association. As it enters the second century of its life new tensions make themselves felt.

For one thing we have come to the end of an epoch in which a very large number of girls have been educated in girls' schools of marked individuality where they have been taught mainly by women, though by no means entirely. There have for a long time been mixed staffs in girls' schools to an extent almost unknown in boys'. Now co-education grows apace. As comprehensive schooling increases and small units are amalgamated to form large ones, many single-sex schools disappear, and it is remarkable how often even the name of the girls' school is lost while that of the boys' is retained in the title of the new unit. At times the process is motivated as much by the economics of

ROYAL COUNTY OF BERKSHIRE

EDUCATION ACTS, 1944 to 1968

NOTICE IS HEREBY GIVEN that in accordance with the approved plan for the re-organisation of secondary education for Newbury, St. Bartholomew's Grammar School and Newbury County Girls' Grammar School will, if the under-mentioned proposals are approved, be amalgamated to form one comprehensive school for pupils of both sexes having an age range mainly from eleven to eighteen years.

(a) THE BERKSHIRE COUNTY COUNCIL, BEING THE LOCAL EDUCATION AUTHORITY FOR THE ADMINISTRATIVE COUNTY OF BERKSHIRE PROPOSE TO CLOSE NEWBURY COUNTY GIRLS' GRAMMAR SCHOOL SITUATE IN ANDOVER ROAD, NEWBURY IN THE COUNTY OF BERKSHIRE.

(b) THE GOVERNORS OF NEWBURY, ST. BARTHOLOMEW'S GRAMMAR SCHOOL (CONTROLLED) PROPOSED TO ENLARGE THE PREMISES OF THEIR SCHOOL SITUATE IN ENBOURNE ROAD, NEWBURY IN THE COUNTY OF BERKSHIRE AND TO CHANGE THE CHARACTER OF THE SCHOOL TO THAT OF A COMPREHENSIVE SCHOOL FOR 1,260 PUPILS OF BOTH SEXES HAVING AN AGE RANGE MAINLY FROM ELEVEN TO EIGHTEEN YEARS.

Notice of Closure of a Girls' School in the process of *reorganization.*
(By permission of the Director of Education for Berkshire)

a situation as by conviction of the value of co-education, just as it was after 1902. Even in the independent sector a number of boys' public schools toy with the idea of co-education or cautiously experiment, though sometimes their reasons are not absolutely clear. "... We are determined," wrote the head master of Marlborough after a small number of girls had been recruited into the sixth form, "that Marlborough should remain a boys' school: as one member of the Council put it 'Marlborough remains a boys' school, but it is a better boys' school for having girls in it'."!

The trend is towards a pattern of secondary education in large mixed schools, although, since it is undeniable that some young people flourish best in small and in single-sex ones, it is to be hoped that some of both will survive the pressures of fashion and reorganization. The pattern has clear advantages, both educational and social, but also enough potential dangers to provoke here two questions. Is there in it a continuing role for head mistresses or could their numbers dwindle to vanishing point? Could certain aspects of girls' education, important and valuable in themselves, be lost?

As schools become bigger and fewer there is keener competition for headships and at the present time markedly fewer opportunities for women to be appointed to them because of the tradition that mixed schools should have head masters with women subordinate in the hierarchy. If this tradition should become more deeply entrenched and accepted, great impoverishment in education would result. As far as girls are concerned, though it is not of course suggested that in schools under head masters the interests of girls would be neglected, they might be undervalued and consistently regarded as rather less important and needing less attention than those of boys. No good could come out of a system by which young people were educated in communities where this occurred, or where women and—by implication—girls were clearly assigned to the second class. It would be positively harmful to future relations and balances in society, and one does not have to be stridently feminist to realize this. Nor is it a symptom of prejudice to believe that in some at least of the cases where well-qualified women have applied for headships of mixed schools, and men have been appointed, there has been discrimination against women.

The blame for this state of affairs is freely put upon women themselves and some of it they must accept. "Women are not appointed to headships," say local authorities and governors defensively, "because good applicants are not forthcoming." There is indeed a scarcity of women of the right calibre, whatever the reasons may be; family commitments; a preference for the pastoral side of teaching rather than the ladder of promotion; or an unconscious lack of confidence inherited from the past. But one thing is certain. This is a time when it should be accepted policy that headships of mixed schools should be equally and genuinely open to women as well as to men. There can be no doubt of their competence. This is demonstrated by those head mistresses who are in charge of large mixed schools—there were sixty-eight of them in the Association in 1972—and who successfully combine the techniques of management with the skill in personal relations and with the concern for individuals without which no school can flourish. But if the opportunities for responsibility are there, women must be prepared to compete for them and not be content with "poverty of aspiration." Otherwise their influence could so diminish that serious flaws in education would result.

One of these could be a lack of understanding of the way in which girls approach their studies at the secondary stage, which is different from that of boys. They are naturally more inclined towards an imaginative approach to subjects, particularly but not, of course, solely towards historical and literary studies. They project themselves more readily into personalities and characters, they are more interested in human relationships and the human side of knowledge. This difference of approach—and it is a difference, not an inferiority—is commonly acknowledged by educators to be a welcome factor which enriches the experience of pupils and teachers, adding as it were, another dimension to learning and teaching. Yet there are some mixed schools where it is not sufficiently understood and here girls do not flourish or achieve their full potential. Derek Miller of the adolescent unit at the Tavistock Clinic was aware of this danger when he wrote, "Girls respond badly in a fundamental way to an educational system which sees their needs as being like those of boys plus cooking. . . . They can be badly affected by educational environments which force them to be academic at the expense of being creative and imaginative," or those, he might have added, where they perceive that their interests and aspirations are not genuinely valued. In order to create an environment where there is a true balance of needs and interests and a fruitful use of differences of approach the presence and influence of women as well as of men is obviously essential. It is not, however, enough for them merely to be present on the staff in sufficient numbers. They must be as fully involved as men in planning and responsibility.

It is natural that head mistresses whose influence on education—and not only on girls' education—has been out of all proportion to their numbers, should be concerned about these matters. They believe that the question of how they shall exert that influence in the future is a crucial one. Certainly it will be in new ways and through different channels, perhaps not so much through a small compact body, as now, but by closer links with other teachers' associations and by joint hammering out of policies, methods and publications more closely related and agreed than at present. To some this might seem the end of an independence highly prized and steadily asserted, but at a deeper level it would be an end only in the sense in which T.S. Eliot wrote:

To make an end is to make a beginning.[1]

There are many people who lament the losses that have occurred in the changes and transitions of recent times, but few would desire to "restore old policies or follow an antique drum" if that should mean a retreat into the past. So much lies ahead which demands constructive planning and liberal thinking, humanity and wisdom that it would be unprofitable to lament too long. We need, it is true, a continuing regard for the best of the past. We need also an unswerving determination to contribute positively to the future, to the making of a society not narrowly egalitarian but diverse and compassionate. With all this in mind we come to the end of the first hundred years of the Association and "the end is where we start from."

[1] *Little Gidding.*

APPENDIX I
Head Mistresses at the Uppingham Conference, 1887

A.S. Ambler	Gravesend High School
A.C. Andrews	Maida Vale High School
M.I. Beal	St Elphin's, Warrington
D. Beale	Cheltenham Ladies' College
M. Belcher	Bedford Endowed High School
M.E. Bishop	Oxford High School
M.M. Blackmore	Roan School, Greenwich
S.M. Burnett	St Catherine's School, Guildford
F.M. Buss	North London Collegiate School
E. Cannings	Shrewsbury High School
E.A. Cocks	Redland High School, Bristol
J. Connolly	Aske's School, Hatcham
A.J. Cooper	Edgbaston High School
E.E.M. Creak	King Edward's High School, Birmingham
E. Day	Manchester High School
E. Day	Grey Coat Hospital, Westminster
E.C. Dugdale	Loughborough Grammar School
M.A. Dugdale	St Anne's, Abbots Bromley
E. Easton	Darlington High School
L.G. Eaton	Preston High School
F.K. Firth	Bath High School
F.M.A. Gadesden	Blackheath High School
F.A. Gilbert	Guernsey Ladies' College
I. Graves	Higher Tranmere High School, Birkenhead
E. Gray	Durham High School
S. Green	Dudley High School
S. Hadland	Milton Mount College, Gravesend
H.M. Jones	Notting Hill High School
F. Lawford	Camden School, London
N. Lückes	Hereford High School
A. Luxton	Brighton High School

F.J. McCallum	Woolwich High School
G.I. Masson	Middlesborough High School
M.A.A. Minasi	Highbury High School
L.M. Monro	Stamford School
M.I. Mowbray	Winchester High School
D. Neligan	Croydon High School
E. Nicholson	Blackburn House, Liverpool
M.J. Nimmo	King Edward's School, Aston, Birmingham
A.A. O'Connor	Clapham High School
A.L. Parmiter	Grammar School, Bath Row, Birmingham
M.E. Pope	Jersey High School
M. Porter	Bedford Modern School
G.C. Rundell	Kendrick School, Reading
K. Rutty	Burton-on-Trent High School
E.S. Shakspeare	Maria Grey School, London
M.E. Skeel	Nottingham High School
K.H. Street	Perse School, Cambridge
I.C. Thomas	Sydenham High School
K. Vokins	Bolton High School
A.D. Vyner	Wallasey High School
A. Wallis	Richmond High School
R.C. Westmacott	Eaton Square High School
M.C. Whyte	Sutton High School
M. Williamson	Princess Helena College, Ealing
E. Woodhouse	Sheffield High School
M.A. Woods	Clifton High School

APPENDIX II

Presidents and Chairmen of committee and other members honoured as Vice-Presidents and Life Members, 1874-1974

The president is elected by the Association. The chairman is elected by the Executive Committee on the nomination of the president, to whom she serves as deputy. The date given is that of election to office.

	Presidents	*Chairmen of Committee*
1874	F.M. BUSS, North London Collegiate School	
1895	D. BEALE, Cheltenham Ladies' College	H. MORANT JONES, Notting Hill High School

1897	H. MORANT JONES	E. DAY, Grey Coat Hospital, Westminster
1899	E. DAY	J. CONNOLLY, Aske's School, Hatcham
1901	J. CONNOLLY	F. GADESDEN, Blackheath High School
1903	S. BRYANT, North London Collegiate School	M.S. BENTON, South Hampstead High School
1905	F. GADESDEN	M.J. MOWBRAY, Winchester High School
1906		M.S. BENTON
1907	E. WOODHOUSE, Clapham High School	M.S. WALKER, Roan School, Greenwich
1909	S.A. BURSTALL, Manchester High School	R.M. HAIG BROWN, Oxford High School
1910		E.H. MAJOR, East Putney High School
1911	M.A. DOUGLAS, Godolphin School, Salisbury	A.B. BRAMWELL, Eltham High School
1913	M.E. ROBERTSON, Christ's Hospital	R. OLDHAM, Streatham Hill High School
1915	A.E. ESCOTT, Sheffield High School	F.R. GRAY, St Paul's Girls' School
1917	R. OLDHAM	L.A. LOWE, Leeds Girls' High School
1919	E.H. MAJOR, King Edward's High School, Birmingham	G. FANNER, Putney County Secondary School
1921	G. FANNER	E.R. GWATKIN, Queen Mary High School, Liverpool
1923	F.R. GRAY	E.M. TANNER, Bedford High School
1925	B.M. SPARKS, Cheltenham Ladies' College	E. STRUDWICK, City of London School
1927	L.A. LOWE	M.D. BROCK, Mary Datchelor Girls' School
1929	E. ADDISON PHILIPS, Clifton High School	D.E. DE ZOUCHE, Wolverhampton High School
1931	E. STRUDWICK, St Paul's Girls' School	I.M. DRUMMOND, North London Collegiate School
1933	M.D. BROCK	M. DAVIES, Streatham County Secondary School

1935	E.R. GWATKIN, Streatham Hill High School	E.A. JONES, Clapham County Secondary School
1937	E.M. TANNER, Roedean School	A. CATNACH, Putney County Secondary School
1939	D.E. DE ZOUCHE	M.S. SMITH, Sydenham High School
1941		M.F. ADAMS, Croydon High School
1942	A. CATNACH, Putney County School, Mayfield	
1944	M.S. SMITH, King Edward's High School, Birmingham	L.E. CHARLESWORTH, Sutton High School
1946	M.F. ADAMS	M.J. BISHOP, Godolphin and Latymer School
1948	L.E. CHARLESWORTH	K.M. REYNOLDS, Park School, Preston
1950	M.J. BISHOP	K. ANDERSON, North London Collegiate School
1952	H. LISTER, Selhurst Grammar School, Croydon	E.M. HUXSTEP, Chislehurst County Grammar School
1954	K. ANDERSON	D.N. GLENDAY, Clifton High School Bristol
1956	A.M. BOZMAN, Manchester High School for Girls	A.F. BULL, Wallington County School, Carshalton
1958	D.N. GLENDAY	M.B. AMBROSE, Dudley High School
1960	A.F. BULL	E.G. HAROLD, Haberdashers' Aske's Acton School
1962	R.N. PEARSE, Mary Datchelor Girls' School	P.R. BODINGTON, South Hampstead High School
1964	D. READER HARRIS, Sherborne School for Girls	B. WILLIAMS, Reigate County School
1966	P.R. BODINGTON	E.J. ATKINSON, Northgate School for Girls, Ipswich
1968	B. WILLIAMS	J.F.R. WILKS, King Edward VI High School for Girls, Birmingham
1970	J.R. GLOVER, Sutton High School	M.R. GRAY, Godolphin and Latymer School
1972	J.R.F. WILKS	M.N. BLAKE, Selby Grammar School

During the twenty years of Miss Buss's presidency, it was customary to honour other members as vice-presidents. Once the biennial succession became established, all past presidents on retirement as head mistresses have become life members. In addition to these, the Association from time to time elects other distinguished members to life membership. The date given is that of election as vice-president or life member.

Vice-presidents

1878	M.E. PORTER	Chelsea High School
1880	S. HADLAND	Milton Mount College, Gravesend
1882	E. DAY	Manchester High School
1883	D. NELIGAN	Croydon High School
1888	A.C. ANDREWS	Maida Vale High School
1889	A.J. COOPER	Edgbaston High School
1890	A.A. O'CONNOR	Clapham High School
1892	E. HASTINGS	Wimbledon High School
1895	A. OTTLEY	Worcester High School

Life members

1907	A.S. HITCHCOCK	Kensington High School
1916	E. ARMSTRONG	Dame Alice Owen's School, Islington
1918	C.E. RIGG	Mary Datchelor Girls' School
	H.M. SHELDON	Sydenham High School
1921	G. McCROBEN	Wakefield High School
1924	B. HEWETT	Walthamstow County High School
1925	M.K. BELL	Sutton High School
1926	M. COLLIN	City of Cardiff High School
	E.M. LEAHY	Croydon High School
1927	M.E. ROBERTS	Bradford Girls' Grammar School
	C.E. AINSLIE	George Watson's Ladies' College, Edinburgh
	M.S. YOUNG	Haberdashers' Aske's School, Hatcham
1928	H.L. POWELL	S. Mary's College, Lancaster Gate
1931	A.M. STONEMAN	The Park School, Preston
	C.L. MORANT	Parliament Hill School, London
1937	A.R. MORISON	Francis Holland School, London
1939	E.A. JONES	Clapham County Secondary School
1943	L.E. SAVILL	Lincoln High School
1946	M.G. CLARKE	Manchester High School
1948	M. DAVIES	Streatham County Secondary School
1952	A. DRUMMOND	Holly Lodge High School, Liverpool
1954	W.M. CASSWELL	Edgbaston High School, Birmingham
1962	M.C. SHARP	Enfield County School

1966	E.M. HUXSTEP	Chislehurst County Grammar School for Girls
	M.R. PRICE	Milham Ford School, Oxford
1969	E.G. HAROLD	Haberdashers' Aske's School, Acton
1971	H.E. VIDAL	Kesteven and Sleaford High School
1973	M. MILES	Mayfield School, Putney

APPENDIX III
Secretaries of the Association

1874-1901	LOUISA BROUGH
1902-1933	RUTH YOUNG
1934-1939	M.E. MARTIN (ex-head mistress of Normanton High School)
1939-1943	GLADYS DURDEN SMITH
1944	MRS CLARK
1944-1946	ETHEL A. JONES (ex-head mistress of Clapham County Secondary School)
1946-1960	JEAN McF. MILLER
1961-	LUCILE SPALDING

APPENDIX IV

Organization of the Association of Head Mistresses Incorporated 1896

Registered Office: 29 Gordon Square, London WC1H 0PU
Secretary: Miss L. Spalding, MA

Membership
The Executive Committee has power to elect as:

1 Ordinary Members, head mistresses of public secondary schools which are recognized as efficient by the Department of Education and Science.
2 Associate Members, retired head mistresses who have normally been in Ordinary membership for at least ten years.

Life Members are all past presidents who have ceased to be eligible for Ordinary Membership and such other members who for distinguished services to the Association are nominated by Executive and elected by the Association at an Annual General Meeting.

In addition, the Executive Committee has power to elect as Affiliates men and women who carry similar responsibilities to those of Ordinary Members but are not eligible for Ordinary Membership, such as a head master or a temporary acting head mistress of a girls' public secondary school or the chief assistant mistress of a mixed public secondary school under the headship of a man.

Honorary Officers
1 The President is elected by the Ordinary and Life Members to hold office for two years. She presides at the Annual General Meeting and Conference and at meetings of the Executive Committee.
2 The Chairman of the Executive Committee acts as deputy to the President; she is nominated by the President and appointed by Executive annually, but in practice she normally holds office for the same two years as the President.
3 The Treasurer is elected annually by the Annual General Meeting.

Branches:
The Association is divided into thirteen Branches. These are:

I	London	VIII	West of England
II	Yorkshire	IX	Six Counties
III	Northern Counties	X	Norfolk and Suffolk
IV	South East	XI	Essex
V	North West	XII	Wales
VI	Midland	XIII	Scotland
VII	East Midland		

In addition there are non-Branch members in Northern Ireland, Eire and in a number of countries overseas.

The Executive Committee
The affairs of the Association are conducted by an Executive Committee which meets regularly six times a year. It consists of the Officers, the Vice-Presidents (past Presidents who are still Ordinary members), not more than five co-opted members, eight General Representatives elected by the Ordinary and Life Members of the Association as a whole, and a number of representatives (27 at present) elected by the Branches in proportion to the size of their membership. Elected members normally serve for a period of two years. Associate and Life members may be co-opted on sub-committees of Executive and, if so, may take part in meetings of the Executive committee but may not vote.

Committees
Standing Committee: Finance and General Purposes.
Sub-committees: Careers, Education, Examinations, International, Salaries and Pensions.
Advisory and Consultative Committees: Constitution, Membership, Parliamentary and Legal, President's Advisory.

Scholarships and other charitable funds administered by the Association
1 Arnold Power Scholarship Fund, "to help towards the education of girls in domestic science, household management, secretarial work or some other subject which will equip her to earn her own living."
2 Careers Aid Fund, "to help a girl in financial need who is taking up

either university or some form of training" and "to help' with the education of girls in cases of need."

3 Amy Bull Fund. This fund was set up by Amy Bull during her presidency: she keeps in personal touch with many head mistresses who retired some years ago on inadequate pensions and whose needs are now pressing.

4 Theedam Aid Fund. This fund is mainly used to help elderly, retired teachers who are in need.

Index